THE YEAR IS 1851

THE YEAR IS 1851

By

PATRICK HOWARTH

COLLINS
ST JAMES'S PLACE, LONDON
1951

PRINTED IN GREAT BRITAIN
COLLINS CLEAR-TYPE PRESS : LONDON AND GLASGOW

To

MY FATHER

whose own father was born in 1851

ACKNOWLEDGMENTS

I OWE much to the kindness of the many people who have helped me with suggestions, criticism and information in the preparing of this book. Most of all I owe to my wife, who has helped me unremittingly.

Among the others to whom I am principally indebted are Mr. J. S. Watson, Fellow of Christ Church, who brought his expert knowledge to bear on many passages of the book; Mr. C. H. Gibbs-Smith, Keeper of Museum Extension Services at the Victoria and Albert Museum, a recognised authority on the Great Exhibition, who made many helpful suggestions; Sir Robert Witt, who most courteously enabled me to study a part of his great collection; the staff of the *Picture Post* Library, the British Museum, and the public libraries of Westminster, Kensington and Chelsea, who were continuously helpful; Mr. Buchanan of Heywood Hill's bookshop in Curzon Street and Mr. Rayward of Goulden and Curry's bookshop in Tunbridge Wells, who brought a number of books to my attention; and Miss Patricia Sadie, who in two minutes suggested a better title for this book than I could find in several months.

The portrait of Metternich is reproduced by gracious permission of His Majesty the King; those of Georgiana, Duchess of Devonshire and Elizabeth, Lady Foster from the Devonshire Collection by permission of Chatsworth Estates Company; for permission to reproduce the remainder, I am most grateful to the National Portrait Gallery, the *Picture Post* Library and the Victoria and Albert Museum. The tables in the text have been taken from Mayhew's *London Life and the London Poor* and *The Times* of 1851.

7

CONTENTS

PART THREE

The Exhibition of 1851

ILLUSTRATIONS

INTRODUCTION

THIS book is an experiment in the technique of the scrap-book. It is primarily an attempt to portray life as it was lived in one particular year of the past. Explanations are, of course, offered of how and why the circumstances and habits which prevailed in that year came about, for otherwise the account would be meaningless. The form is not, however, that of a narrative advancing from stage to stage, nor is the book a portrait of a reign or of a generation. It is an attempt to make history stand still in one particular year, much as in a different way a series of photographs will make it stand still, and the central event described is one which, to a remarkable extent in that particular year, dominated people's minds.

The year chosen is 1851, and the central event is that spectacle which became known to contemporaries and posterity simply as the Great Exhibition. After the passage of a hundred years, this event is still considered to be of sufficient consequence for it to be celebrated to-day, in a spectacular fashion, by the decision of a Government which was not conspicuous for its tendency to look to the past for inspiration.

The Great Exhibition is now far enough removed in time for us to be able to view the events which were contemporaneous with it dispassionately. Until fairly recently the portrayal of the Victorian age, either in whole or in part, was strongly influenced by that process of action and reaction which has such a marked effect on the relations between parents and children. People will violently repudiate or, if their temperament inclines them that way, violently embrace the beliefs of their parents' generation for emotional and personal reasons. To a lesser extent they may have strong emotional reactions to the beliefs of their grandparents, but beyond that point passion tends to become dissipated. There are no doubt people alive to-day who were alive when the Great Exhibition was held, but personal recollections of the event must be almost negligible. Already many people—probably most people—will find, if they examine the matter, that those of their forebears who could have visited the Great Exhibition were dead before they themselves were born.

Fashions in opinion on the products of the Victorian age are, of course, still changing. The belief, which at one time seemed well established, that nearly all Victorian products were ugly, has already been out of date in certain circles for years. There are knowledgeable critics who now state that Butterfield should be regarded as a neglected genius ; Victorian pub interiors enjoy something of a vogue, particularly as film sets ; and Victorian silver is esteemed by connoisseurs. This process of changing fashion will certainly continue. Charles Reade or George Eliot, Disraeli or Kingsley, Meredith or Surtees—any of these may at any time in the foreseeable future be the resuscitated novelist of the moment. However, the iconoclastic delight in debunking the Victorians can never again be what it was, nor indeed can the delight of the subsequent reverse process. Just as it is no longer daring to assail the Victorians, so it is no longer daring to champion them. We can only approach the age of all except the late Victorians with calm, and with the benefits and disadvantages which calm bestows.

This calm now enables us to assess with some objectivity the value of the picture of the Victorian age which, as a result of all that has been written and painted, photographed and acted on the subject, has become crystallized in the minds of millions of people who have no personal Victorian memories. This assessment may cause us to accept or reject the greater part of the popular picture according to our point of view. What is difficult to refute, however, is that, whereas many of the least attractive of the familiar Victorian pictures—such as Dotheboys Hall or the driving of children under six to work in coal mines—belong rather to the first ten years of the Queen's reign, those peculiar virtues—tinged perhaps with some associated vices—which posterity has come to accept as typically mid-Victorian were already in general evidence by the time of the Great Exhibition.

By 1851 the curious blend of immediate optimism associated with the freeing of trade and of ultimate doubt occasioned by the theory of evolution had already made its mark. By 1851, too, Lord Palmerston had had a prolonged stretch as Foreign Secretary, and the immensity of Britain's wealth and her unique position among the nations were generally recognised. The middle classes were in the ascendant, and so were their views on chastity and their taste in interior decoration. Samuel Smiles had learnt, though not yet fully elaborated, his doctrine of self-help; the Gothic revival had begun ; and most of the numerous political and literary giants of the reign had already made their mark.

Historians have usually placed the end of the early Victorian and the beginning of the mid-Victorian periods somewhere about the death of the Prince Consort in 1861, or even later. A less misleading point of division might, however, be found in the year 1848, when the Chartists were defeated, and the triumph of free trade had begun to be accepted as certain. On that reckoning the Great Exhibition must be regarded as a mid-Victorian event, and it is perhaps permissible to consider it the first great pageant of the mid-Victorian world. Certainly it was the mid-Victorian world—within which the Great Exhibition may be included— and not the aftermath of the Regency at the beginning of the Queen's reign, nor the *fin-de-siècle* era at its end, which brought into being the picture which posterity normally conjures up when it hears the word " Victorian."

The later Victorian Forsytes, those of the generation of Soames and Young Jolyon, tended to think of the age of the Great Exhibition as an enviable one of both prosperity and certainty, however much they might chafe at some of its conventions. In the nineteen-twenties and nineteen-thirties it became almost obligatory to challenge this picture and to associate, for instance, the mid-Victorian paterfamilias with the hypocrisy of a Pecksniff or the tyranny of an Edward Moulton Barrett ; in the same period the collection of ludicrous Victoriana became a pastime first of the witty and then of the precious. How we who are now in the middle of the twentieth century will react to the same subject is not yet clear. One purpose of this book is to recreate the world of the Great Exhibition sufficiently vividly for individual judgments on its qualities to be formed.

Part One

THE
HISTORICAL BACKGROUND

CHAPTER ONE

ENGLAND WHEN VICTORIA BECAME QUEEN

T HE England of 1837, the year of Queen Victoria's accession to the throne, presents extraordinary contrasts, when seen in retrospect, with the England of the Great Exhibition of 1851. The picture which we who look back now are likely to form of both worlds, that of 1837 and that of fourteen years later, is largely one of a society trying to adapt itself to the demands of the Industrial Revolution. However, it is in the very difference of adaptability to that revolution that the contrast between the two ages becomes most apparent.

The Industrial Revolution has been happily named. Those movements which can properly be classified as revolutions do more than simply change the manner in which power is exercised. They are distinct from *coups d'état* and brawls between factions in that they shatter a whole social structure, and a new social structure is something which is not easily created. The immediate sequel to a revolution is generally a period of maladjustment : its benefits are seldom conveyed to the first generation which follows it ; and one of the qualities of a revolution, whether social or aquatic, is that in the ensuing calm there is a tendency for scum to settle at the top.

The Industrial Revolution did not of course take place all at once ; indeed as a world-wide movement it is still clearly in being. However, its consequences were sufficiently rapid and widespread for a violent transformation of England to have occurred in the early part of the nineteenth century, and it was a peculiar misfortune of the first Victorians that the social structure which they inherited was not very well fitted to absorb the shock.

The Government at the beginning of the Queen's reign was still of the kind which had been found suitable for ruling a largely agricultural and unshifting population, at the head of which had stood a nationally powerful aristocracy and a locally powerful squirearchy. Five years after the outbreak of the French Revolution an English Attorney-General had been able to state that it was high treason for anyone to agitate for representative government, which he had described as " the direct contrary of the government which is established here." It is true that the Reform Act of 1832 had widened the electorate, but it had not extended the privilege of voting to those who were not property owners.

Whether a representative government could have been formed in the eighteen-thirties which would have dealt adequately with the major social problems of the time is an academic and perhaps unprofitable question. What is certain is that the Governments which did exist were by their very traditions limited in their capacity for dealing with wholly new problems.

As far as the party affiliations of Governments were concerned, the first thirty years of the century had been a period of Tory predominance. The Tory vote had been one means by which the limited electorate could express its disapproval of the principles and excesses of the French Revolution and could subscribe to a belief in old institutions, which Burke had comfortingly likened to old boots. When the Tories went out of power and the Whigs came in for prolonged stretches, there were indeed changes, but those who immediately benefited from the changes were the manufacturers and not the rapidly increasing urban proletariat.

The nature of the national finances in the early Victorian period gives some indication of what a Government was then expected and empowered to do. The question whether there should or should not be an income tax, for instance, remained a matter for serious dispute down to the time of the Great Exhibition. The tax had originally been introduced as a wartime measure to sustain the struggle against the forces of Napoleon, and when it was reimposed during a time of peace in Europe there was a general outcry, the tax being denounced as an intolerable means of intrusion into gentlemen's private affairs and an inducement to dishonesty

The tax upon property

in merchants. An attempt by the Government in the forties to raise the rate of income tax from 7d. to 1s. in the pound had to be abandoned because of the strength of the opposition to it, and three years before the Great Exhibition the first speaker to follow the Chancellor of the Exchequer in the budget debate demanded ample time for consideration " before giving consent to a proposition so important as the renewal of the income tax."

Such revenue as there was came largely from the import duties, particularly the duties on timber and sugar. The import duties on corn, which became politically of supreme importance in the forties, were fiscally relatively unimportant in the thirties. An additional source of revenue, which may seem surprising to the student of modern economics, was the export duties. Nevertheless, in spite of the complexity of the means by which revenue was brought in, its total was remarkably small, and even in the year of the Great Exhibition the national budget amounted only to some fifty million pounds.

With such limited resources no Government could have embarked seriously on the kind of social legislation which posterity has come to accept as indispensable to the well-being of all industrial societies. The most important event which did occur in the field of social legislation in the thirties was the Poor Law Amendment Act, which came into force in 1834. This was a conscientious attempt to regularise the system or lack of system by which relief to paupers had been administered in the past. The old methods had been untidy and had conferred immense powers of patronage on the administrators. Under the new system the administration was put in the hands of responsible persons chosen by the ratepayers and controlled by three Poor Law Commissioners.

The recipients of relief, however, who had relatively little interest in the tidiness or untidiness of the administration, mostly regarded the whole measure with resentment and even hatred. One of its basic principles was that able-bodied persons were entitled to relief only after they had been admitted to workhouses. However, the general dread of the workhouse and the difficulty of providing the necessary workhouse accommodation combined in practice to prevent the application of this principle in many parts of the country. The forbearance shown by the administrators of relief in not abiding by the regulations too rigidly,

Able-bodied persons were entitled to relief only after they had been admitted to workhouses

and the fortuitous circumstance that for two years after the passage of the act the price of corn happened to be low, were probably responsible for the fact that demonstrations against the new Poor Law were not more violent than they were.

Although it may seem clear to the modern economist that for the growing pains of an industrial society the only satisfactory anæsthetic is increased social legislation and, therefore, increased governmental expenditure, early Victorian economists generally held different views. The economic theory of laissez-faire—scornfully described by Kingsley as " the Great King Laissez-faire "—was a cult to which most people who considered the matter were emotionally as well as intellectually attached ; and the liberation of trades and industries from taxes was, in a number of cases, effected in practice as well as advocated in theory.

Thus in 1830 the beer tax was abolished, with a result which Sydney Smith described by saying : " Everybody is drunk. Those who are not singing are sprawling. The sovereign people are in a beastly state." Sixteen years later a much more important restriction was lifted when the Corn Laws were repealed.

It was with this structure of a largely aristocratic Government elected on a limited franchise, a paltry national revenue, and ineffectual social legislation, that early Victorian England had to contend with the effects of the Industrial Revolution.

Technologically the Industrial Revolution consisted of a number of inventions and discoveries which gave new power to machines, which in their turn created and helped to satisfy a new demand for coal. Sociologically, therefore, the movement made its earliest and deepest impressions in the towns. Resistance to the possibilities of mechanisation in agriculture remained strong for years in England as in other countries, and the early nineteenth century's reluctance to accept agricultural machinery seems as surprising as its resistance to artificial fertilisers.

The social structure of the countryside was indeed changing. Many small farmers or yeomen were giving up agriculture, some of them selling up and investing in industry. Enclosures were still being effected, although less speedily and extensively than at the end of the eighteenth century, and the fact that no Poor Law relief was administered to property owners drove many people from the land in times of depression. However, the changes which were taking place in the countryside were not comparable in magnitude with those which were taking place in the towns.

The sudden growth in economic importance of the industrial towns coincided with an astonishing increase in the population. The census which was made every ten years showed that in the first half of the nineteenth century this increase occurred at a fairly steady rate of some two million people per decade. It was only partially due to the higher number of births ; much of it must be attributed to far-reaching improvements which had occurred in medical science. There was a lower death-rate in infancy, small-pox was largely conquered, drainage was improved, and scurvy nearly disappeared. A very real factor in bringing about a considerable improvement in general hygiene was, too, the large-scale manufacture of cheap cotton shirts.

Whatever the causes may have been, the increases in population occurred with special rapidity in the manufacturing districts. In Lancashire, the centre of the cotton industry, the population rose by 98½ per cent in only thirty years, and in Monmouthshire in the same period the increase was 117 per cent.

This growth in the population of the towns was caused by migration as well as by natural increase, and it was this very movement, the drift from the countryside to the industrial towns, which created the most difficult social problems of the early Victorian age. The towns were hopelessly ill-equipped to provide for their new surplus populations, who could be housed only in conditions of slumdom with wholly inadequate public services. In Edinburgh poor persons who fell sick were actually committed to prisons from motives of humanity ; Engels estimated that in Manchester 7,000 people were served by only thirty-three lavatories ; and in the forties *The Times* was writing of " the fetid drain, the cesspool, the crowded convict-hulk, the damp, ill-ventilated abodes in which too many of the population pass their lives."

Industries which attracted large sections of the population by offering opportunities of employment and therefore some means of subsistence were mining, metallurgy, cotton and the railways. Mining and metallurgy were old industries which were being revitalised ; thus the deep sinkings of the thirties made possible much of the large coal output of the forties. Cotton spinning by means of machines was a newer industry, and railways —at least the kind along which locomotives ran—were a nineteenth-century creation. All expanded enormously in the forties.

It would not be true to state that the development of these industries in the early Victorian period was left to private enterprise without any protest from responsible quarters. The belief that the railways should be nationalised, for instance, was expressed by politicians long before the creation of the party which ultimately put this proposal into effect. In 1836 Lord Londonderry advocated that after the repayment of capital and interest the railways should revert to the public ; the Duke of Wellington regretted the modest extent of State control over the railways which the Act of 1840 permitted, while at the same time complaining that the railways were killing the stage-coaches ; and Gladstone proclaimed that " nothing in the nature of what is called a vested interest " ought to be recognised as attaching to the railways. In 1845 Gladstone even introduced a measure which obliged the railway companies to run at least one train a day over their systems with third-class accommodation at 1d. a mile. These trains came to be known as the parliamentary trains.

Road versus rail, 1845

Gradually, however, the principles of laissez-faire and the argument that over-centralisation was essentially un-English prevailed. The railway companies were generally allowed to acquire the powers they sought, and already in the mid-forties George Hudson, the railway king who was later to be ruined when the frauds in the management of the Eastern Railway were exposed, was being fêted in the most exclusive circles. Indeed, when he was returned as Conservative M.P. for Sunderland in 1845, the news was sent to London by a special train which achieved a speed of 75 miles per hour. In view of the fact that the electric telegraph was established on a high proportion of the railways by that time, this may strike us to-day as a curious extravagance.

The railway kings were only one of a new class of industrial magnates. Even more powerful in their control over the lives and deaths of their workers were the mine-owners and mill-owners, and attempts to limit the extent of the control which they could exercise were halting, sporadic, and for a long time ineffectual. It is true that trade unions could indulge in a certain amount of legal activity after the Combination Act of 1799 had been repealed in the eighteen-twenties : Lord Ashley, the great reformer, entered the House of Commons a quarter of a century before the Great Exhibition; and the principle of factory legislation began to be accepted in the thirties. Nevertheless in 1832 the only industrial concerns in which children received any legal protection were the cotton mills, and even in them children of nine could be made to work for twelve hours a day. Moreover, in the early days of factory legislation

George Hudson, the railway king

cotton manufacturers could publicly demand sympathy by complaining that their industry was singled out in unfair discrimination.

If we are to look back from a modern viewpoint and apply those standards of morality and even of long-term political expediency which the great majority accept to-day, we can hardly fail to condemn the rule of the early captains of industry in England as brutal and senseless. Some historians have attempted to whitewash their conduct, and others, by focusing attention on the experiments of exceptional employers such as Robert Owen, have distorted the picture of the whole ; but apologies of this nature are probably little more than exercises in ingenuity. Certainly the public conscience did not have to wait until the twentieth century before expressing its horror at the conditions which prevailed in mines and factories in early Victorian England. Expressions of horror came readily enough from the succeeding generation, a generation which had been instructed by the findings of a number of uncompromisingly truthful Royal Commissions and the imaginative literature to which these findings partly gave rise.

Then it was learnt that children who were employed in the coal-mines as hurriers had leather belts slung round them with a chain attached

Children had leather belts slung round them with a chain attached so that they could pull loads

and passed between their legs so that they could pull loads ; that a six-year-old girl could be regularly forced to carry half a hundredweight of coal on fourteen long journeys daily ; that fathers ruptured themselves in lifting loads of coal on to their children's backs, and that in the mining districts what appeared to be a new race of diseased and permanently crippled creatures was being raised, creatures who became worn-out old men and women by the time they reached their thirties.

The Industrial Revolution did in fact confer a new kind of power on a new kind of potentate, and history, both before and since that time, is full of examples of how ruthlessly power of this kind is habitually exploited. Mellowness and forbearance in the exercise of authority came no more and, probably, no less naturally to the industrial magnate in the eighteen-thirties than they do to the political functionary in the one-party State of to-day.

It would of course be wrong to suppose that the new industrial magnates differed fundamentally from other sections of the well-to-do in their understanding of the respective rights of the employer and the employed. The separate existence of the two nations, as Disraeli described the rich and the poor, was accepted as an inescapable fact as readily by the land-owning aristocracy as it was by the newly enriched industrialists. When Lady Cavan's tenants in the early thirties agitated for an increase in their weekly wages of nine shillings, Baron Alderson, sitting in judgment, declared that they had not been respectful and should have trusted in the proved benevolence of their superiors. Not having trusted in this benevolence, a number of them were sentenced to hard labour. In comparable terms the humanitarian Wilberforce, who at the same time relentlessly pursued his campaign against the iniquities of the slave trade, stated that it was incumbent on the poor " faithfully to discharge its duties and contentedly to bear its inconveniences."

The prevailing mood of the ruling classes, of the aristocrats who figured so prominently in the Governments and also of the leading churchmen, was not conducive to the earnest consideration of questions of social reform. Earnestness was not indeed a characteristic of the age. In their very dress the leading figures in society revealed a certain frivolity and a distaste for that sombreness which has been *de rigueur* among public figures ever since. Hair was scented, and jewellery and gay waistcoats were common ornaments. Disraeli as a young man even wore rings over his white gloves, although it is true that he had that tendency towards sartorial extravagance which the English then, as in the days of Whistler and Wilde, considered more easily pardonable in a foreigner than in one of their own people.

Lord Melbourne, who was Prime Minister when Victoria became Queen, may reasonably be regarded as an exemplary political figure of the first years of the Victorian age. Posterity—at least in so far as it is represented by modern anecdotists and scenario writers—has taken a benevolent view of Melbourne. One reason for this may be that he was such a strikingly different type from his successors who flourished in the mid-Victorian world of prosperity and decorum. His wit, for instance,

THE HOME OF THE RICK-BURNER.

Rick-burning as an expression of agricultural discontent continued to be fairly common

was unrestrained by any considerations of prudery ; the persecutions of the Norton family made him face allegations of sexual promiscuity in the Law Courts ; his wife, from whom he separated, was a novelist with an unconcealed infatuation for Byron ; and the story was told of him that,

William Wilberforce

when he was searching for a suitable recipient for the order of the Garter, and it was suggested that it might be conferred on himself, he replied that he could not see what he would gain by taking his own bribe.

Melbourne's evident human weaknesses, his manners, which seem to belong to the Regency period, and his paternal solicitude for the young Queen, have made an attractive figure of him in retrospect. Nevertheless, an examination of his political career reveals neither oratorical nor administrative gifts of distinction, and his tendency towards personal laziness was matched by a political philosophy, which suggested that inaction was generally better than action.

There were, it is true, political figures in the years immediately preceding and immediately following the Queen's accession who both advocated a policy of social reform and received some degree of public recognition. One such was Robert Owen, who was born in 1771, and who survived the Great Exhibition. It is difficult, however, to avoid the conclusion that though as an individual capitalist Owen was singularly successful, as a social reformer he was at the best a glorious failure. At the age of nineteen he became manager of a cotton mill which employed five hundred workers, and his factory in New Lanark well deserved to be regarded as a model. His experiments in communal living, however, in Hampshire, in County Clare and in Indiana all ended in disaster. Whereas Ashley, the Conservative peer and devout Anglican, who was born thirty years after Owen, and who moved with the main stream of mid-Victorian reform, left behind him a series of major legislative achievements, Owen, the early Victorian socialist and antagonist of established religion, left as his principal monument a legend. For some years before his death he was chiefly interested in spiritualism, and his sons all became citizens of the United States.

Early Victorian England, in short, faced the convulsions of the Industrial Revolution with a social structure which was an uneasy survival from a less disturbed age. The politicians had little inclination to make sweeping changes ; the economists believed in the operation of what were regarded as natural laws ; the industrialists were rapidly piling up their own fortunes ; and the churchmen were largely concerned with good living. Reviewing these circumstances, the observer, looking back after more than a hundred years, may well wonder why the whole structure did not collapse in an upheaval of violence.

The same problem was frequently in the minds of contemporary observers. Engels was not alone in believing that a bloody revolution was imminent in 1846. During the thirty years which followed the Napoleonic wars fear of a revolution was a more constant source of worry to the English well-to-do than it has been in any subsequent period.

One of Robert Owen's villages of union

Chartist riots in Newport

There were plenty of disturbances to provide grounds for this fear. With the advent of peace after the war with France, the unemployed, whose numbers had grown unusually large, held seditious meetings with increasing frequency. They even continued the practice, which had immortalised the name of a Leicestershire half-wit and given the word " Luddite " to the English language, of destroying the machines which they regarded—not without reason—as their personal enemies.

Destruction of machinery became less frequent in the thirties, but rick-burning as an expression of agricultural discontent continued to be fairly common. There were riots associated with the agitation for the Reform Bill, in spite of the fact that the Bill which was demanded, and which was eventually passed in 1832, could have enfranchised hardly any of the rioters. Nottingham Castle was set on fire, and mobs broke into the Bristol Mansion House and got drunk on the contents of its cellars.

Violent expressions of popular discontent became less sporadic and more purposeful in the late thirties and the early forties. In many industrial towns, particularly in the North of England and in the Midlands, factory workers gave expression to their grievances in acts of violence. The police station in Manchester was sacked, and there were riots in Stoke and Halifax, Bolton and Rochdale, Stockport and Blackburn.

During the forties too the movement known as Chartism was steadily gaining in strength. The programme of the Chartists, as set out in their manifesto, was confined to parliamentary and electoral reform. All their demands in this respect have by now been satisfied except that which called for annual elections to Parliament. One demand indeed has been more than fulfilled, for in the matter of the franchise they advocated only total adult male suffrage.

However, the People's Charter became a slogan with a ready popular appeal. People could sing about it, with little adaptation of the original words, to the tune of " Rule Britannia," and the very concept of a charter provided an emotional rallying-point for the large disaffected sections of the population. Chartism was not, however, a well-disciplined political movement. It had an organisation of " classes " and " leaders," with

The Chartist meeting on Kennington Common

propaganda being carried on by "missionaries," but these were terms
borrowed from the Methodists.   Methodist and Evangelical influences
were indeed apparent in policy as well as in phraseology : many of the
leading Chartists were fervent advocates of temperance and thrift, and
a number of youthful ministers of religion were bold enough to admit
allegiance to the Chartist cause.

The movement, though inspired by a consciousness of social injustice,
was not in fact a socialist one.   Its acknowledged leader, O'Connor, was
by no means an orthodox socialist, and it is significant that his hatred of
the Whig aristocracy led him to instruct his followers to vote for a number
of Tory candidates in the 1841 election.   Chartism can be regarded rather
as a partially articulated expression of discontent, of that feeling which
led to the riots of 1831, the rick-burning and the destruction of machinery.
It was a sane embodiment of the feeling which drove various lunatics to
indulge in a spate of successful or attempted assassinations.   Daniel

Hamilton's attack on Queen Victoria. The Queen had
a number of close escapes

*The trial of Daniel McNaughten, whose name is perpetuated in the
famous rules on murders by lunatics*

McNaughten, for instance, whose name is perpetuated in the famous
rules on the subject of murders by lunatics, killed Peel's private secretary
in 1843, when it was the Prime Minister himself who was the intended
victim, and the Queen herself had a number of narrow escapes.

The very fact that the name " Chartist " was not confined to a hard
core of fanatical revolutionaries, but was claimed by the shiftless and
illiterate, the Irish immigrants who helped to undercut wages, and the
rest of a real Lumpenproletariat, was responsible in part for the fiasco
with which the movement came to an end on April 10th, 1848. When
the final showdown was due to take place, less than five per cent of the
half-million who were due to assemble on Kennington Common appeared ;
the Government proved to be extremely well informed of intentions by
agents provocateurs ; the monster petition was found to be signed with
names such as " Mr. Punch " and " Victoria Rex " ; and the demon-

strators did not even cross the Thames. When " God Save the Queen "
was sung in the streets of London that night there was a general instinctive
feeling, which proved to be correct, that the danger of violent political
revolution in England had come to an end.

There was, indeed, a striking abruptness in the manner in which the
movement to overthrow the existing order in England collapsed. A widespread inclination towards revolution does not, however, disappear
overnight simply because a mass demonstration has failed. Its eradication
must be a gradual process, and in the England of the late forties that
process was to a large extent the modification of the social conditions
from which the revolutionary movement took its impetus.

It is, of course, possible to exaggerate the evils of the social conditions
in England in the thirties and early forties. Some observant foreign
travellers, following, for instance, Baron Meidinger—who stated that
Ireland was the only part of the United Kingdom in which he had found
rural poverty and backwardness comparable with that to be seen in
many parts of Germany, Switzerland, France, Spain and Italy—considered
conditions in England relatively prosperous.

The social background at the time of Queen Victoria's accession was,
moreover, that which has been preserved for us in the *Pickwick Papers*.
The world of Pickwick, the world in which the stage-coach came to its
final glory, may seem on a first impression to be an extraordinarily joyous
one. It is a world of hospitality and bonhomie, to which the term
" conviviality " is appropriately and repeatedly applied. It seems wholly
natural in this world for Wardle, a simple country gentleman, to invite
all four Pickwickians on a very brief acquaintance for a week of glorious
entertainment ; for Jingle at the cricket match to find beer by the hogs-
head, beef by the bullock and mustard by the cartload ; and, wherever
they go, for Tupman to find amiable women, Winkle to find vigorous
sportsmen, and Snodgrass to find amateur poets. Moreover, there is
as much hilarity in the lives of Toby Weller, the coachman, and Sam
Weller, the boots, as there is in those of the relatively well-to-do Pickwickians, and many of the social institutions which are ridiculed are not
portrayed as causing active unhappiness. There is plenty of corruption
but not much depression in the Eatanswill election, and there is something
invigorating in the manner in which the Pickwickians are attacked

Charge of the 3rd Dragoon Guards during the Bristol riots

by an angry mob when it is suggested that they may be informers.
However, there is even in *Pickwick* a continual undercurrent of
implied social misery. The Stroller's Tale gives an appalling picture of
theatrical poverty and of the host of " shabby, poverty-stricken men "
who " hang about the stage of a large establishment." The citizens of
Muggleton, who had presented 1,420 petitions against the continuance of
negro slavery, took care to present an equal number against any interference with the factory system at home. Even the benevolent Pickwick,
when considering the Kentish towns, recorded that " a superficial traveller
might object to the dirt which is their leading characteristic " ; and,
when engaged in rook shooting, he was " not quite certain but that the
distress of the agricultural interest, about which he had often heard a
great deal, might have compelled the small boys attached to the soil to
earn a precarious and hazardous subsistence by making marks of themselves for inexperienced sportsmen."

It is true that the *Pickwick Papers* are less evidently a biting indict-
ment of contemporary social conditions than are the novels of Dickens
which followed. There is, for instance, no institution in *Pickwick* quite
like that of Wackford Squeers. However, to deduce from this that social
conditions were better when *Pickwick* began to appear than they were
when Dickens wrote *Nicholas Nickleby*—or indeed when he wrote *David
Copperfield*, the last of his novels to appear before the year of the Great
Exhibition—would be to deny the evidence not only of other contemporary observers, but also of Dickens himself. In the preface which he
afterwards wrote to the *Pickwick Papers*, Dickens commented on the
important social changes which had taken place " almost imperceptibly
since they were written." These changes affected, among other things,
the conduct of elections, legal procedure, the Poor Law and public health.
The greatest of the changes could be summarised in the expression of a
new confidence that fever and consumption would not for ever " be let
loose on God's creatures."

There was, indeed, a change which had the effect of greatly altering
the emphasis in Dickens's treatment of social problems. This change was
not, however, in the social conditions themselves but in Dickens's awareness of their significance, and in this respect his works were a revealing
reflection of contemporary opinion.

This increasing awareness of social problems, which Dickens so clearly reflected, was one of the forces which gave rise to the new society which was coming into being in England by the time the Great Exhibition was launched. The story of how this new society was formed ; how the Anti-Corn Law League triumphed where the Chartists failed ; how social legislation came to be recognised as a necessary function of Government ; how trade and industry flourished so that the Exhibition was intended and accepted as an example to a troubled Europe of the prosperity and security of Britain ; the story, in short, of how the mid-Victorian world was brought into being by change, but not by violence, is one of the most absorbing which can engage the attention of the historian, the sociologist, or anyone else who is concerned with the problems of the growth of modern society.

CHAPTER TWO

THE NEW SOCIETY

W HEN the Prince Consort died ten years after the Great Exhibition was held, *The Times* in a sincere and ringing eulogy stressed the debt which the nation owed him for " the happy state of our internal polity, and a degree of general contentment to which neither we nor any other nation we know of ever attained before."

By 1861 the expression of such opinions on the general welfare of the nation had long since ceased to be a novelty. They were, indeed, being voiced a very short time after the removal of any danger of a Chartist rising. Less than six months after the Chartist fiasco on Kennington Common, *The Times*, reviewing the thirty-three years which had elapsed since the end of the Napoleonic wars, could declare : " Those 33 years have been a period of unexampled prosperity, happiness and improvement. We have enjoyed the longest peace on record."

The claim that the country had enjoyed an uninterrupted period of peace could be disproved by anyone who considered what had been happening outside Europe, and the " unexampled prosperity " must have been imperceptible to many people who could not afford to buy *The Times*, which then cost fivepence. It is, however, significant that a newspaper could make a comment of this nature in the year 1848 without apparent fear of contradiction. The change of outlook on contemporary events, which it indicates, goes some way towards both illustrating and explaining the remarkable fact that the England which gave rise to the Chartist movement and the monster petition of 1848 also gave rise to the Great Exhibition and all it stood for in 1851.

44

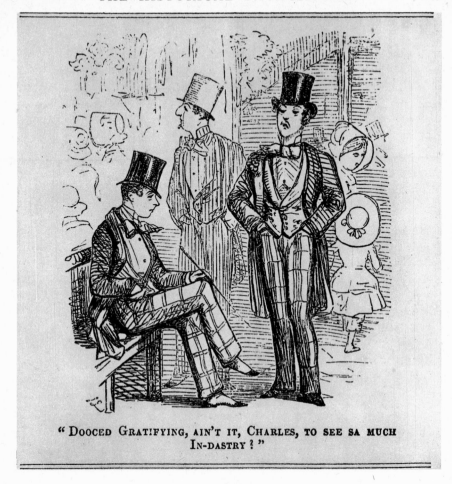

"Dooced Gratifying, ain't it, Charles, to see sa much In-dastry?"

A wave of almost unexampled prosperity crossed the country

Great changes were, indeed, taking place in England in the middle and late forties, and it is perhaps characteristic of the period that there was both a widespread awareness of the existence of these changes, and a prevalent belief that the changes themselves were nearly all for the better.

The evidence of numerous writers can be cited, who were both aware that they were living in a rapidly changing world and convinced that mankind was benefiting in consequence. As a commentary on social conditions, there is a striking parallel between the preface which Charles Kingsley wrote to later editions of *Alton Locke* and Dickens's preface to the *Pickwick Papers*. Stating that the passages on Cambridge in *Alton Locke* were based on his own memories of the years 1838-1842, Kingsley wrote :

" For thirty years past, gentlemen and ladies of all shades of opinion have been labouring for and among the working classes, as no aristocracy on earth ever laboured before ; and do you suppose that all that labour has been in vain ? That it has bred in the working classes no increased reverence for law, no increased content with existing institutions, no increased confidence in the classes socially above them ? If so, you must have as poor an opinion of the capabilities of the upper classes, as you have of the lower."

Elsewhere in the same work Kingsley declared that " return to the system of 1800-1830 is, I thank God, impossible," and the evidence of Lord Ashley, a more effective social reformer than Kingsley ever was, bears out this opinion. The steady increase in the amount of attention which the ruling classes were prepared to devote to social problems was one of the developments which most constantly cheered Ashley in the course of his ceaseless crusade. His private diary continually bears witness to this. Thus in 1843, commenting on a speech which he had just made in the House of Commons on education, he wrote : " Could this have been effected a few years ago ? Such a speech would have been heard with cool indifference or shouts of derision."

Disraeli, too, a more acute political observer than Ashley, noted the same trend. When discussing the spirit of the age in *Sybil ; or the Two Nations*, which was written in 1845, he stated : " We live in an age in which to be young and to be indifferent can be no longer synonymous."

The change in the prevailing attitude towards social problems, of which there was such a general awareness, is reported by different contemporary writers as having occurred at different stages in the early part of the Queen's reign. Its occurrence is also ascribed to a variety of causes. However, those who believed that Almighty God had manifested His goodness by purifying men's hearts, and those who thought that there had been a general betterment of mankind in consequence of the new material progress and prosperity, nearly all had one thing in common : they subscribed to what was in effect a new feeling of optimism, a feeling which was an essential part of the spirit which inspired the Great Exhibition.

It is comparatively rare in human history for optimism to be widespread among thoughtful commentators on current affairs, and we may well wonder why it suddenly became so prevalent in the years immediately preceding the Great Exhibition. Whatever conclusions we may come to, we must, in making an analysis, take two movements into consideration. In some ways these movements were divergent and even antagonistic, yet they were not altogether disconnected. One movement took the form of a rapid spreading of the benefits of trade by the removal of outmoded fetters. The other movement was less consciously controlled, but it was certainly no less powerful : it may be described as a concentration of scattered moral forces brought to bear on social problems which urgently demanded settlement. The repeal of the Corn Laws was a stage in the first movement, the Evangelical revival was an instance of the second.

The history of English political life in the forties is largely the story of the triumph of the Anti-Corn Law League and the failure of the Chartists. The expressed object of the Anti-Corn Law League, which grew out of the association founded by Cobden in Manchester in 1838, was to agitate for the removal of the import duties on corn. The League achieved victory in 1846, when the duties were greatly reduced, and it was enacted that they were to be almost eliminated in three years' time.

However, the League expressed something more than merely a demand for revision of one particular aspect of fiscal policy. It represented the growing belief that the natural consequence of free trade was peace between nations, and that, once he had achieved these two ideals, man's opportunities of progress were boundless. This was the principle which inspired Cobden, the chief architect of the League, throughout his political career. After the repeal of the Corn Laws he devoted a great deal of his energy to advocating a general reduction of armaments, and he toured Europe triumphantly in the cause of free trade or, in his own phrase, " as first Ambassador from the people of this country."

Politically the League became one of those movements which periodically occur in English history, and which cut across and interfere

Meeting of the Anti-Corn Law League in Exeter Hall

with the working of the two-party system. The liberal tradition gave it a natural affinity with the Whigs, but it was a Conservative Prime Minister, Sir Robert Peel, who in 1846 introduced the measure for which the League had so long been agitating. Fundamentally the League was at variance with both the Conservative and Whig parties, for neither, as it was constituted in the forties, truly represented the element from which the League drew its main strength, the middle classes of the new industrial towns.

The League did, indeed, make a point of attracting working-class recruits by political propaganda which was in general more skilful than that of the Chartists.

John Bright and Richard Cobden

Its members delighted, too, in rich, vituperative language when they exposed the sins of landowners, whose "venison," they said, was "sweetened with widows' tears." There was even a temporary alliance in 1842 between extremist elements in the League and extremist elements in the Chartists. Nevertheless, the leadership of the League was at all times predominantly middle-class, moderate according to its own lights, nonconformist and northern. Cobden was the son of an unsuccessful southern farmer and was a member of the Anglican Church; he found prosperity, however, in a business career in Lancashire. Bright, who was in many ways more typical personally of the element which gave the free trade movement its strength, was a Lancashire Quaker and also a successful business man. He delighted in political conflict, and exhibited the same gusto and the same brilliant oratory when campaigning against capital punishment and flogging in the Army, as he did when promoting the cause of free trade. Lord George Bentinck said of him that if he had not been a Quaker he would have been a prize-fighter.

The campaign of the Anti-Corn Law League was not only politically successful. The events of the years immediately following its triumph seemed to vindicate the League's most extravagant claims. Shortly after the Corn Laws were repealed a wave of almost unexampled prosperity crossed the country.

There were a number of different causes of the economic boom in England at the end of the forties. Among the chief of them were the new means of distribution, which the railways had provided, and the markets which British goods were then enjoying overseas. Official figures for the year 1851 gave the value of exports as £197,309,876 and of imports as £100,460,433. It is true that the figure for imports was based on out-of-date and often misleading prices, but, even when allowance for this has been made, the picture of prosperity which the figures reveal is clear enough—particularly to Englishmen of the mid-twentieth century, to whom an adverse balance of trade seems almost inescapable.

A great stimulus to the British export trade was provided by the discovery of gold in California in 1848. The importance of this discovery was not, it is true, immediately apparent to many English people. Even relatively enlightened newspapers could comment that experience was " against the presumption that California . . . will prove a real benefit to the United States," and " we see little to regret that the region is not ours." However, it was not long before the newly created purchasing power in the United States was fostering an insistent demand for British goods, and at the same time the real increase in wealth which the technological advances of the Industrial Revolution offered was beginning to be more and more widely felt.

The immediate reason why the Government in power had accepted the proposal that the Corn Laws should be repealed was that this seemed the only way of providing cheap bread to relieve a terrible famine in Ireland, which had followed from a failure of the potato crop. In England too, as well as in Ireland, the years 1846 and 1847 had been regarded as years of economic and financial difficulties. Wheat had had to be imported from America and Russia ; a partial failure of the American cotton crop had had a serious effect on Lancashire's manufactures; and in 1847 there had been a number of bank failures. However, by 1851 such economic and financial disasters seemed to superficial observers to have

A great stimulus to the British export trade was provided by the discovery of gold in California in 1848

come to an end. Prices, too, had come rocketing down, and although it was a fact that the prices of many other commodities fell more sharply than did the price of grain, the reduction in the cost of living was unhesitatingly claimed as a further justification of the League's policy. Economists in general, and the spokesmen of Manchester in particular, apparently had good reason for claiming a greater part in shaping the policy of Her Majesty's Government. *Punch* depicted the protectionist as a member of one of a number of recently extinct races; another was that of the coachman.

In contrast with the free trade movement, the movement which aimed at social reform by the protection of the exploited classes was forwarded by a number of differing and even conflicting factions, not one of which was so skilfully organised or so immediately successful as the Anti-Corn Law League.

During the forties the educated public received a steady stream of information on the ways in which the less fortunate sections of the English people had to live. The provision of this information was not on the whole resented. *Punch* found it worth while to publish Hood's plaintive and horrifying " Song of .the Shirt " in its Christmas number of 1843 ; Dickens's novels enjoyed tremendous popularity as soon as they appeared ; and even Friedrich Engels found an English public by contributing to such publications as Owen's *New Moral World* and the Chartist *Northern Star*.

This new awareness of the realities of social conditions was followed by a number of measures designed to effect a general improvement. Factory legislation continued, and the Act of 1847 virtually established the practice of the $10\frac{1}{2}$-hour day. A serious attempt to better the health of the nation was made with the Public Health Act of 1848. A real improvement in the Poor Law was afforded by the Poor Removal Act in 1846, which made it no longer necessary for poor relief to be administered in the parish in which the recipient was born ; and local government became steadily more responsible and more effective after the passage of the Municipal Corporations Bill in 1835. Democratic local government was not, however, extended to rural districts until nearly fifty years later, when county councils were established. Serious attention was also being given to the need for State-financed education, although progress was limited by continual sectarian squabbles on the subject of religious instruction in the State-financed schools. Finally, in 1851 Ashley introduced a Bill " to encourage the establishment of lodging-houses for the working classes," a measure which Dickens described as " the best Act ever passed by an English legislature."

The effects of legislation of this kind may seem, by comparison with what later generations were to demand, to have been somewhat limited.

PUNCH'S MUSEUM OF EXTINCT RACES.

Punch *depicted the protectionist as a member of one of a number of recently extinct races; another was that of the coachman*

However, by the time the Great Exhibition was launched, there were no women working in the coal-mines, and there was already established in Whitehall that Board of Health whose importance as an instrument of government was reflected in the varied powers exercised by the Ministry of Health until this year. The concern with public health shown in the forties by men such as Chadwick had indeed a lasting effect in shaping the structure of English local and central government ; without it the curious anomaly, whereby the Ministry of Health was for many years responsible for housing, could hardly have come into being.

The taking of measures to improve social conditions was, moreover, being considered in the forties less and less as the exclusive privilege of the more benevolent members of the ruling classes. Associations formed by working men to fight for their own rights and to protect each other were gaining in strength. The pretentiously named Grand National Consolidated Trades Union, which had been formed in 1834, and which had soon claimed half a million members, had collapsed because it had been an ill-organised mass movement with no effective driving power. After 1845, however, there was a revival of union activity, and as each union confined its interventions to single or to kindred trades, a new strength was gained by the very concentration on limited objectives. It was in the year of the Great Exhibition that a union, which has now developed into one of the chief forces in industrial politics, the Amalgamated Society of Engineers, was formed.

Another form of association which steadily gained in strength in the forties was that of the friendly or benefit societies, such as the Great Western formed by railway workers in 1838, and the Hearts of Oak formed in 1841. Friendly societies combined the advantages of a form of mutual insurance with the ceremonial trappings of robes and oaths, which secret and semi-secret societies have offered almost since man became articulate. Their attraction in an age in which there was in existence such a curious amalgam as a Communist Church was considerable ; and some impression of the strength of working men's associations can be gained from the fact that, three years after it came into being, the Miners' Association could pay William Roberts £1,000 a year to conduct its legal business.

The early development of co-operatives also dates from the second half of the forties. It was in 1844 that a group of poor men, mostly flannel workers, collected £28 and opened a co-operative shop in Toad Lane in Rochdale, and their success was quickly and widely infectious. The leaders of the co-operative movement in its early stages tended to keep aloof from controversial politics, and the fact that consumers' co-operatives were normally used only by those who could save at least £1 put them beyond the reach of the lowest strata of the population. Nevertheless, by the end of the forties the development of co-operatives had already become one of the main points in the programme of the Christian Socialists.

These two movements which have been discussed, the one which led towards free trade and greater opportunities for capitalist enterprise, and the other whose end was the protection and uplifting of the labouring classes, were certainly divergent movements. Modern conventional socialism suggests that they were movements in wholly opposite directions, and the theory which gave rise to this point of view is, of course, defensible, particularly if purely economic standards are applied. Nevertheless, there were very real links between the forces taking part in these move-

The first English co-operative shop

ments, and it is just these links which reveal some of the unique characteristics of the period.

The common meeting-ground between the supporters of Cobden and
his Anti-Corn Law League and the supporters of Ashley and his Factory
Acts which was most familiar to both was a moral and religious one. It
may perhaps be best described as the practical application of the teachings
of John Wesley—that is to say, the philosophy which inspired the
Methodist movement among Nonconformists and, to an almost equal
extent, the Evangelical movement in the Anglican Church.

Most of Wesley's better known sayings, such as that about cleanliness
being next to godliness, and his instruction to " get all you can, save all
you can, give all you can," had been such as might be uttered by Government public relations officers in the modern era ; and it was a characteristic
of both the Methodist and the Evangelical faiths that they offered an
unusually satisfying formula for combining social obligations with
personal advantage.

The moral revival which Wesley had propagated in the preceding
century carried away Englishmen of all classes and denominations in the
eighteen-forties. There was indeed at the same time a purely religious
revival, which was expressed with both grace and learning in the Oxford
Movement, and which induced enthusiastic young members of that
University to deliver *Tracts for the Times* at country vicarages. The
Oxford Movement, however, appealed primarily to intellectuals, and was
largely an expression of the feeling that there was a need for greater
mysticism in men's lives. It had much less powerful social effects than
the Evangelical revival, which was in the first instance a movement of a
moral rather than a religious nature.

It became fashionable some years ago to scorn the moral force which
was inherent in Evangelicism. It is easy enough to condemn it to-day
as a means whereby a steadily increasing number of people combined
enjoyment of large incomes with absolute confidence in their ability to
pass the entrance tests into the Kingdom of Heaven—and this in spite
of the warnings given by the founder of their religion of the difficulties
of bringing off such a long-priced double. However, whether we despise
it or admire it, we can hardly deny that it was this peculiar moral force
which so largely shaped English society in the years immediately pre-

Thomas Chalmers. "Whatever the calls may be which the poverty of a human being may have on the compassion of his fellows, it has no claim whatever on their justice"

ceding the Great Exhibition. It was this force which gave rise to much of the legislation which paved the way for modern state socialism, and it was at the same time a force which permeated the movement towards free trade and the extension of capitalism.

Opposition to the newly awakened social morality was still outspoken in certain quarters in the forties. The voices of those who had attacked Owen, when he suggested that children under ten should not be made to work, with the argument that there was a danger of their acquiring vicious habits through want of regular occupation were still to be heard. The demand which Malthus had made on thinkers " formally to disclaim the right of the poor to support " found an echo in the writings of the Scottish religious leader, Thomas Chalmers, who in his *Christian and Civic Economy of Large Towns* stated : " Whatever the calls may be which the poverty of a human being may have on the compassion of his fellows, it has no claim whatever on their justice." When the Public Health Act of 1848 was being discussed, the *Economist* declared : " Suffering and evil are nature's admonitions. . . . Impatient attempts of benevolence to banish them from the world by legislation . . . have always been more productive of evil than good."

The moral revival was, however, strong enough to resist warnings of this nature, and the career in the House of Commons of Lord Ashley, which ended in the year of the Great Exhibition, when he entered the House of Lords as the seventh Earl of Shaftesbury, was an undeniable example of how much a man of integrity, guided throughout by the principles of Evangelicism, could at that time achieve.

It was no belief in democratic principles which inspired Ashley in his long career as a social reformer. In so far as he troubled to consider the subject, he was antagonistic to political democracy, and he opposed the Reform Bills of 1832 and 1867. His ideal of government was an authoritarian one, whose justification must be a constant adherence to moral principles. This attitude was clearly expressed on one occasion in Parliament, when he declared : " Let the State but accomplish her frequent boast ; let her show herself a faithful and pious parent." Ashley regarded himself as morally dedicated to a political career, and indeed he had done so ever since, at the age of fourteen, he had seen a group of drunken coffin-bearers carrying away the earthly remains of a pauper. He had

The Earl of Shaftesbury.   An example of how much a man of integrity, guided by the principles of Evangelicism, could achieve

thereupon determined to devote his life to uplifting the down-trodden and oppressed.

Social reform was, in Ashley's opinion, inseparable from the Protestant faith, which faith he considered to be most properly expressed by the Evangelicals. He was as deeply concerned with the problems of religious instruction in the Ragged Schools and the establishment of an Anglican bishopric in Jerusalem as he was with conditions in cotton mills and coal-mines.

It is a revealing commentary on both of them that Ashley and Dickens, in spite of the virtual absence of humour from the one and the abundance of humour in the other, were friends and mutual admirers. Both were deeply aware of social injustices, and the means of alleviation which each of them recommended were similar. Dickens has sometimes been criticised by twentieth-century socialists for the fact that, having analysed the social conditions of his day in incomparable fashion, he could offer no more satisfactory solution than the kind of *deus ex machina* represented by the Cheeryble brothers. It was however just this panacea envisaged by both Dickens and Ashley, namely the exercise of power and charity by those who were inspired by strong moral principles and the Protestant faith, which brought about the major social reforms of the period in which they lived.

The Protestant moral revival, which was expressed in their daily lives by authoritarians such as Ashley and free-traders such as Bright, did much more to ameliorate social conditions than revolutionary movements such as Chartism had done, although it is true that the Chartist agitation served to give the ruling classes a salutary fright. Apart from the legislation to which it gave rise, the moral revival directly affected the conduct of those who were controlling the nation's affairs. There was, for instance, a steady elimination of corruption from Government : the idea of corruption was as distasteful to Peel and Gladstone as it was understandable to Melbourne, and Sir John Shelley was already out of date when in 1845 he described Lord John Russell as " that most rare of all beings, a truly honest politician."

The Church, too, benefited from the new mood of society, not only in added prestige, but also in a marked improvement in the personal conduct of its representatives and in its internal organisation. One

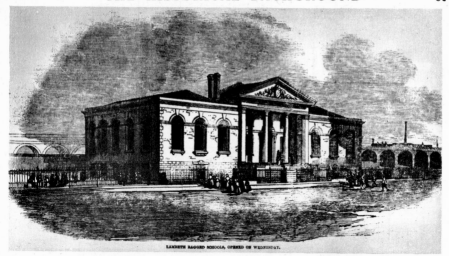

LAMBETH RAGGED SCHOOLS, OPENED ON WEDNESDAY.

Ashley was deeply concerned with the problems of religious instruction in the Ragged Schools

effective instrument for reform was provided in the shape of the Ecclesiastical Commission, which was established to revise the incomes of episcopal sees and to make suggestions for the creation of new ones, and the moral authority of the Church was greatly enhanced by the work the Commission did in removing abuses.

Social reforms and a higher standard of integrity in Church and Government can reasonably be claimed as assets, of whose presence Britain could legitimately boast by the time the Great Exhibition was launched. Whether the corresponding reforms which occurred in social manners and the habits of daily life are also to be considered as assets must be a matter of opinion.

Among the most striking changes in social habits, which occurred in England within a few years of Queen Victoria's accession, were a great increase in the regard shown to the outward forms of religion, and the acceptance of more rigid standards of propriety. The church sermon grew into one of the central features of the week's activities : books of sermons became best sellers, and Gladstone, for instance, even delivered a lecture on the subject of preaching. Family prayers, which had been something of a rarity at the beginning of the century, became a regular part of the routine of most upper and middle-class households.

That these standards of propriety, which the respectable English were beginning to accept in the forties, were indeed new ones was emphasised by a number of contemporary writers, including the extremely observant Thackeray. In an address to the readers of his own day, for instance, he wrote : " Do not be frightened, ye fair readers of the present day ! We are not going to outrage your sweet modesties, or call blushes on your maiden cheeks." Then, commenting on fashionable society of a hundred years earlier, he added : " But 'tis certain that their ladyships of Castlewood never once thought of being shocked, but sat listening to the parson's funny tales until the chapel bell, clinking for afternoon service, summoned his reverence away for half an hour. There was no sermon. He would be back in the drinking of a bottle of Burgundy."

Thackeray's verdict was that " manners . . . were looser a hundred years ago ; tongues were vastly more free and easy ; names were named, and things were done, which we should screech now to hear mentioned." It is true that he also wrote of his contemporaries gambling and drinking at Homburg and Baden in much the same way as their ancestors had done at Bath and Tunbridge Wells. However, the comment was cynical and in some ways misleading. The habit of going to the Continent of Europe to indulge in secret dissipation had not yet become widespread among Englishmen of the eighteen-forties and fifties.

The refinement of English manners was not only commented on by observant novelists such as Thackeray, or analysed in detail by the ladies of Cranford ; it also provided a source of livelihood for another class of writers who soon became numerous, the writers of books of etiquette.

England in the forties was confronted by a major problem of social adjustment caused by the rapid growth in numbers and pretensions of the middle classes. Books on etiquette were in consequence found by many to be a necessary guide to a new world of gentility. Meanwhile the public schools, particularly the Rugby which Thomas Arnold refashioned in the thirties, were forwarding the process of converting the sons of manufacturers into gentlemen in one generation—a conversion which, as Alton Locke's cousin discovered, could be completed by the taking of Holy Orders.

The new moral outlook caused rapid and widespread changes of habit in others besides the privileged classes. While the well-to-do were being instructed by books on etiquette and the tradition of the regime to which Tom Brown had had to submit at school, a comparable movement was on foot to refine the habits of the less fortunate classes—a movement in which ministers of religion, both Nonconformist and Anglican, took an active part. Among the many principles which were extolled for the edification of the poor, two in particular had a powerful effect on life in the great industrial towns. One of these principles was a belief in the sanctity of the Sabbath, the other was a consciousness of the evils of alcohol.

Sabbatarianism and temperance reform may be difficult to regard seriously to-day, when the former manifests itself chiefly in the desire of busybodies to deprive us of the obvious benefits of Sunday theatres ; and when drunkenness is effectively quenched by taxation except among some small privileged groups, who live largely on commercial expenses, or are entitled to buy their liquor out of bond. A hundred years ago, however, these two movements had evident social as well as quasi-religious justifications. Belief in the sanctity of the Sabbath was very largely responsible for preventing the advent of a seven-day week in industry, and the temperance movement at least limited the depredations made by cheap liquor on the underfed, uninstructed and spiritually hopeless poor.

Both movements gained continually in strength. The Bill which Sir Andrew Agnew annually introduced with the object of prohibiting all work on Sundays steadily received more votes, and on the subject of drink *The Times* by 1853 could write : " No way so rapid to increase the wealth of nations and the morality of society could be devised as the utter annihilation of the manufacture of ardent spirits."

Joyless Sundays ; a tendency to alternate between the dreary extremes of drunkenness and teetotalism ; and the growth of that middle-class element, which Thomas Arnold's son kept on denouncing as Philistines until the concept seemed to become an obsession with him—these, too, were by-products of the moral revival which occurred in England in the eighteen-forties. They all contributed to the peculiar character which England was acquiring at the time of the Great Exhibition.

Another condition which the England of 1851 enjoyed, and one which differentiated her in some degree from the countries of the European Continent, was a growing sense of peace and security. Whereas revolutions occurred in one country on the Continent after another in 1848, England in that year suffered from nothing more upsetting than the Chartist demonstration on April 10th. Even in Ireland the main disturbance of the year was put down by fifty policemen. There was in Ireland the familiar crop of those incidents which were commonly known as " agrarian outrages "; nevertheless, in the year 1849 the Queen and the Prince Consort visited Ireland, and in the next year it was stated in the Speech from the Throne that " Her Majesty in her late visit to Ireland derived the highest gratification from the loyalty and attachment manifested by all classes of her subjects."

These words would not readily have been uttered during many other phases of Anglo-Irish relations, and they were indicative of the satisfaction with conditions prevailing throughout the Kingdom which English political leaders were beginning to feel. So far as political agitation—or the absence of it—was concerned, this satisfaction was easy to justify. By 1851 the former Chartist demagogue, Bronterre O'Brien, was chiefly occupied with a peaceful movement known as the National Reform League, which merely advocated that the State should purchase land and lease it to the unemployed ; and the Cabinet crisis which lasted throughout a large part of the same year aroused a minimum of public interest.

The belief that after 1848 England was, in contrast with other European countries, a relative haven of security was not confined to Englishmen. In many European countries revolution was succeeded by counter-revolution, so that persons of a wide variety of views were forced to become political exiles ; and it is a revealing commentary on the state of England that, between the first European rising in 1848 and the launching of the Great Exhibition, figures as diverse as Prince Metternich, King Louis-Philippe and Karl Marx all came to England to find refuge.

Louis-Philippe arriving with a week's growth of beard, Metternich installing himself in Richmond as Herr von Meyer, and Marx laboriously pursuing his education in the British Museum, were by no means the only distinguished political refugees England accepted. Louis Napoleon had the distinction of serving as a special constable in the Chartist

Metternich installed himself in Richmond as Herr von Meyer

troubles ; Guizot suffered the indignity of being blackballed from the Athenæum ; and even the future Emperor William I of Germany learnt in England, as he put it, to practise humility.

The fact that it was to this country that political refugees of such different kinds came is not the least important of the circumstances which must be considered by those who would attempt to pass judgment on the England of a hundred years ago. Many other circumstances, however, of equal importance must clearly also be considered, and it would be premature to pass a judgment of any kind in these pages until a closer examination has been made of the wealth and poverty to be found at different levels of society ; of the characteristics of home life ; of the amusements people enjoyed and the art they created ; of the religious and scientific problems which troubled them ; and of the moral and political standing of Britain in the world.

Part Two

THE
WORLD OF 1851

CHAPTER THREE

WHAT PEOPLE COULD EARN AND WHAT MONEY COULD BUY

T HE game of choosing which period of the past one would prefer to live in is an ancient one and has been played by many eminent persons. The distinguished historian of the age of Queen Victoria, Mr. G. M. Young, made an interesting contribution to it when he wrote : " Of all decades in our history, a wise man would choose the eighteen-fifties to be young in."

Thackeray, who may well be considered wise and who was not quite forty when the decade of the eighteen-fifties opened, made a somewhat different comment. Preferring, as he did, to set his romances in the England of a century before, he once wrote : " A rich young English peer in the reign of George the Second ; a wealthy patrician in the reign of Augustus : which would you rather have been ? There is a question for any young gentleman's debating-clubs of the present day."

The difference between these two comments is immediately apparent, yet perhaps they are not quite incompatible. Neither writer was in any case considering the lives of the whole population during the period he eulogised. Thackeray was concerned only with those people who had more money than they knew how to spend, and Mr. Young was probably concerned with those who had opinions of their own and some hope of being able to express them.

We who live in the age following the second World War are likely to approach the subject of the ideal period of the past from an economic standpoint. This is the fashion of our time, and, like most fashions in the writing of history, it puts into the right focus one series of facts while distorting another. Nevertheless, it would be foolish to disregard the fashion entirely, for no judgment we may make on whether or not the time of the Great Exhibition would have been an agreeable one to live in can have any value, unless we have first considered its economic conditions.

In applying economic tests to the eighteen-fifties, we must bear one consideration in mind. This is that man does not judge his own prosperity any more than he judges his own happiness by absolute standards. He judges his prosperity in relation to what he has known in the past, and there was a very marked difference between the economic conditions which many people knew in the forties and those they were to know in the fifties.

By the time the Great Exhibition was launched, the improvement which had occurred in material conditions in the immediately preceding years was being felt at all levels of society. The reduction in the cost of living was particularly noticeable. Based on an index figure of 100 for the year 1790, in 1847 the cost of living figure had been 116 ; in 1850 it was 83. To the poor, in the days before labour was sufficiently organised to insist on higher wages by coercion, the cost of living was an even more important factor in shaping lives than it is to-day.

With the expansion of trade, employment was much more easily found than it had been in the early forties, when Engels estimated the reserve of labour to be about a million and a half persons. When Parliament was opened in February, 1851, it was noted in the Speech from the Throne that " the state of commerce and manufactures of the United Kingdom has been such as to afford general employment to the labouring classes." It is true that this encouraging comment was immediately qualified by the statement : " I have to lament . . . the difficulties which are still felt by that important body among my people who are owners and occupiers of land." However, even the owners and occupiers of land, who were regarded as the main sufferers from the repeal of the Corn Laws, had been considerably assisted by a 6½ per cent loan to tide them over their difficulties.

However, economic betterment is not something which comes to a community suddenly or as the immediate result of any one stroke of

Mr. Punch's Industrial Exhibition of 1850

policy, no matter whether that stroke is the repeal of the Corn Laws, the nationalisation of basic commodities, or any other popular panacea. Consequently, although around 1851 economic conditions had recently changed, and were continuing to change, for the better, it would be wrong to suppose they were violently transformed. The hungry forties having been what they were, there was still at the time of the Great Exhibition, when thousands of admirers were drawn to that monument to human progress, an inordinate amount of poverty and misery to be found among the people of Britain.

By the year 1851 a huge urban proletariat had become an established part of British society. A generation of men and women was growing up in the towns, numbers of whom had literally never seen green fields. Yet the drift from the countryside to the towns, which had been so evident in the thirties, continued at an accelerated pace. The census for the year 1851 showed that approximately half the population of some

†COMPARISON OF THE DENSITY OF THE POPULATION
IN 1841 AND 1851: ENGLAND AND WALES

TOTAL POPULATION, 1851: 17,922,768   TOTAL POPULATION, 1841: 15,884,294

	No. of persons to each inhabitable house	No. of persons to each 100 acres	
		1841	1851
Agricultural Counties			
Lincoln	5·0	21·7	23·8
Rutland	4·9	22·7	25·0
Huntingdon	4·8	25·0	25·0
Cambridge	4·9	30·3	35·8
Essex	5·0	35·7	34·5
Sussex	5·7	32·2	37·0
Hereford	4·8	20·8	18·2
Agricultural and Sub-manufacturing Counties			
Westmorland	5·2	11·6	12·0
Norfolk	4·8	32·2	33·3
Suffolk	4·8	33·3	37·0
Hertford	5·1	40·0	43·5
Bedford	5·1	37·0	43·5
Buckingham	4·9	33·3	31·3
Northampton	4·9	31·2	33·3
Oxford	4·9	34·4	37·0
Berks	5·0	34·4	41·7
Hants	—	47·6	38·4
Wilts	4·9	30·3	27·7
Dorset	5·1	27·7	28·6
Somerset	5·2	41·6	43·6
Devon	5·7	32·2	34·5
Sub-Agricultural and Sub-manufacturing County			
Gloucester	5·3	55·5	26·1

† *Published in* London Life and the London Poor *by Henry Mayhew.*

Manufacturing Counties			
Lancaster	5·8	166·6	200·0
Yorkshire	4·9	42·6	48·7
Chester	5·3	58·8	65·2
Nottingham	5·0	47·6	55·5
Leicester	4·7	43·0	45·4
Warwick	4·9	71·4	83·3
Worcester	5·0	52·6	55·5
Mining Counties			
Durham	5·9	47·6	62·5
Cornwall	5·2	41·6	41·7
Manufacturing and Sub-mining Counties			
Derby	5·0	41·6	40·0
Stafford	5·2	71·4	83·3
Agricultural and Sub-mining Counties			
Shropshire	5·0	28·5	28·6
North Wales	4·9	19·3	19·6
South Wales	5·1	19·0	22·2
Sub-agricultural and Sub-mining Counties			
Northumberland	4·9	21·2	25·6
Cumberland	5·3	18·5	20·0
Monmouth	5·4	43·0	55·5
Metropolitan County			
Middlesex	7·9	1000·0	1059·0
Sub-Metropolitan Counties			
Surrey	6·3	125·0	144·0
Kent	5·7	55·5	63·6

NOTE.—An *Agricultural* county has *more than* 10 per cent, and a *Sub-agricultural* county *less than* 10 per cent of its population employed in agriculture. A *Manufacturing* county has *more* than 15 per cent, and a *Sub-manufacturing* county *less* than 15 per cent of its population employed in manufacture. A *Mining* county has *more* than 5 per cent, and a *Sub-mining* county *less* than 5 per cent of its population employed in mining.

Years	Population England and Wales	Numerical Increase	Increase per cent	Annual Increase per cent
		Annual average increase per cent, 1.41		
		Increase per cent in 50 years from 1801 to 1851, 101		
*1801	8,892,536	2,375,501	37	0·7
1811	10,164,068	1,271,532	14	1·4
1821	11,999,322	1,835,250	18	1·8
1831	13,896,797	1,897,475	16	1·6
1841	15,914,148	1,982,489	14	1·4
1851	17,922,768	1,968,341	13	1·3

*The population at the decennial term, as here given, is the amended calculation of the Registrar-General, as given in the new census tables.

Years	Population Scotland	Numerical Increase	Increase per cent	Annual Increase per cent
		Annual rate of increase per cent, 1.16		
		Increase per cent in 50 years from 1801 to 1851, 78		
*1801	1,608,420	343,040	27	0·6
1811	1,805,864	197,444	12	1·3
1821	2,091,512	285,657	16	1·6
1831	2,364,386	272,865	13	1·3
1841	2,620,184	255,798	11	1·1
1851	2,870,784	245,237	10	1·1

*The returns here cited are copied from those given by the Registrar-General in the new census.

twenty million were already urban dwellers, and an impression of the speed of the drift from country to town can be gained from the fact that less than half of those adults who were registered as Londoners in 1851 were London born.

It was among this shifting population, most of whom had been driven to the cities by want, and who had not yet acquired urban roots, that the extremes of squalor tended to be found. There was, for instance, a huge influx of impoverished Irish into the English and Welsh cities and Glasgow, particularly in the years 1847 and 1848 as a direct consequence of the Irish famine.

Many of these Irish were transported like cattle in boats which brought them to Newport for half a crown a head. In the cities they continued to live to some extent as a race apart. For one thing, they mostly still practised their religion, whereas urban proletarianisation was rapidly followed by godlessness among large numbers of the English ; for another, they showed a greater readiness than the English to accept the very worst of conditions. They were less unwilling to enter the work-houses, and they seemed able to support themselves and their families on even less money. The effect of their competition in the labour market was inevitably therefore to lower wages. Those Irish who were not pre-pared to endure the worst and who had serious hopes of " bettering themselves "—as the contemporary expression put it—tended to emigrate to North America.

The solution which was found to the colossal problem of housing the huge numbers of immigrants into the cities was in itself both an expression and a cause of much of the worst squalor. Apart from those who were admitted to workhouses, the poor were mostly accommodated in what were known as lodging-houses. The workhouses were virtually voluntary prisons, and it is significant that they were given a smaller allocation of soap per inmate than the prisons had ; lodging-houses were considered to be better than the workhouses chiefly because they conferred a greater degree of freedom.

Conditions in many London lodging-houses were still horrifying even as late as 1851, by which time various Board of Health regulations were in force, including one which demanded the whitewashing of walls. Twenty or more human beings commonly slept in the same room, and

" Are You not Irish ? " " Och! no, Ma'am, I'm Carnwall sure ! "

there were frequently a number of dogs as well. A penny less was charged for those who could not aspire to a part share of a bed or a palliasse, and who were prepared to sleep all huddled together on the kitchen floor. The sexes were mingled indiscriminately in the same beds, boys and girls being initiated into sexual practices from the age of ten upwards. The w.c. commonly took the form of a pail in the middle of the room, to which both sexes resorted ; in spite of the Board of Health, bugs could be scraped off the walls in handfuls ; and it was the common practice to get at least half-drunk, as otherwise sleep was found to be impossible.

To live in such a lodging-house was not, however, the worst condition to which the urban poor were driven by economic necessity. Perhaps the worst fate was that of the sweat-shop workers, who saw no hope of ever being able to escape from their bondage. The sweat-shops were not simply a means of making clothes at a minimum cost for a maximum profit ; they were in themselves a complete way of life, one of the most appalling ways of life ever devised.

In the worst sweat-shops the workers lived on the premises. The pay they received was not enough to enable them to buy necessities, and some sweaters, as those who ran the sweat-shops were called, would advance money against the pledge of the workers' clothes. Once such a transaction had taken place, the worker was of course at the sweater's mercy. He was unlikely ever to be able to redeem his clothes, for, though held permanently on the premises and charged exorbitantly for his lodging, he was not even sure of whole-time employment. The most calculating sweaters would, if they had regular work for a dozen operatives, have some three dozen operatives available in order that rush jobs could be completed in time. So the worker remained permanently incarcerated in the sweat-shop, making clothes which were often in practice sold to rich clients by fashionable tailoring establishments. If he had a wife or a family, their best hopes of warding off starvation were likely to be prostitution, other people's charity or the workhouse.

It was just because they offered little or no hope of release that the sweat-shops were probably the worst economic oppressors. However, there were other occupations of the urban poor which, though they conferred a greater amount of freedom, were no more remunerative and every bit as sordid. Numbers of people, for instance, regularly made their living by delving in the rivers and sewers and selling what they could find; these were the dredgers, the sewer-hunters and the mudlarks. There were also more specialised scavengers, such as cigar-end finders and wool-gatherers. Then there were the many costermongers. It was estimated that, whole families included, some 30,000-40,000 people in London alone subsisted from the sale of foodstuffs in the streets, and three or four days' consecutive rain might be enough to bring any of them face to face with the threat of starvation.

Those who made their living in the London streets appear from the descriptions of the great contemporary

THE MUD-LARK.

Delving in the rivers and sewers

social observer who analysed their lives in detail, Henry Mayhew, to have been a colourful lot. Among those he listed were " Irish fruit-sellers; the Jew clothesmen; the Italian organ boys, French singing women, the German brass bands, the Dutch buy-a-broom girls, the Highland bagpipe players, and the Indian crossing-sweepers." However, though colourful, they were nearly all desperately poor, and of course they suffered from perpetual insecurity. The selling of ham-sandwiches in the streets was, for instance, a new and, it might have been thought, profitable trade. Yet Mayhew found a representative ham-sandwich seller who earned only 3s. 6d. a week and who had to pay 2s. a week for his lodging. This man would regularly walk eight miles in order to buy ham at $\frac{1}{2}$d. a pound less than he had to pay elsewhere.

In all the larger industrial towns factory conditions were still for the greater part deplorable. Legislation had done something to mitigate the hardships of women and children, but a twenty-four-hour single shift in mill or factory was still not unknown, and some mills which worked on day and night shifts had bunks in which the children slept, one shift of children going out of the bunks as soon as another shift was ready to go in.

Disease was the natural consequence of the poverty and oppression from which the sub-strata of the urban population suffered. The most devastating scourge was certainly tuberculosis. Statistical evidence of the true extent of its ravages is lacking, but the continual references in contemporary novels—even in those which dealt with genteel life—to "a fell disease," and the statements of observers, who claimed, for instance, that practically all workers in sweat-shops were consumptive, give some impression of how far tuberculosis had spread. As Mrs. Gaskell expressed it in *Mary Barton*, the poor were " fatalists with regard to infection ; and well for them that it is so."

Small-pox, on the other hand, was on the decline as the result of vaccination, and only among the older people were its ravages, particularly in the form of blindness, commonly visible. Typhoid and cholera raged from time to time. There was no serious cholera epidemic in 1851, but there had been an alarming one in 1849. In view of the general sanitary arrangement in the great cities, the prevalence of such diseases was less than might have been expected. As Mr. Peter Quennell has pointed out, the Fleet River, before its diversion underground in the sixties, was really a " common sewer for a population of nearly half a million," and the *Quarterly Review* exposed scandals in the disposal of sewage even in such elegant districts as Belgravia and Kensington.

The conditions which helped to spread infection in lodging-houses and sweat-shops were also directly responsible for much of that depravity among the lower orders, which shocked such well-to-do Victorians as cared to consider the subject. When we consider the extent of the depravity, we may not be altogether surprised at the extent of the shock. The incidence of prostitution to-day, for instance, is negligible in comparison with what it was a hundred years ago. Then it was the natural consequence of extremes of poverty, housing conditions which rendered promiscuity inevitable, and the availability of patrons whose demands were not readily met on their own social level. Treatment of venereal disease was at best sporadic, and there were recorded cases in which prostitutes committed crimes—as, for example, one who deliberately broke windows in St. Paul's churchyard—solely in order to be admitted to prison and, in consequence, to receive some sort of medical treatment.

The cheapness of spirits, the insanitary nature of the water in many cities, and the longing to procure some temporary relief from suffering equally naturally encouraged alcoholism, in some cases at an astonishingly early age. The sight of a five-year-old reeling drunk in a tap-room was not unknown, and in some families gin and opium were regularly administered to the children so that they could be kept quiet while their mothers went to work.

Various kinds of crime were also encouraged by the lodging-house system. Few lodging-house keepers would surrender criminals to the police, and many acted as fences. If a young person appeared at a low lodging-house and had not the twopence or threepence required to pay for his quarters, he might well be told to come back when he had stolen the necessary money.

Depravity as an inevitable consequence of association was a feature of urban rather than rural life, and lodging-houses in small country towns were, as often as not, quite decent places. As regards economic conditions, however, the depths of poverty experienced in rural districts were just as profound as those in the cities.

Charles Kingsley showed, for instance, in *Yeast* that there was a rural counterpart to the picture of urban misery contained in *Alton Locke*. The impression of country yokels which Lancelot gained when he visited a village fair was that " the majority seemed under-sized, under-fed, utterly wanting in grace, vigour and what the penny-a-liners called ' rude health.' " Their food was inadequate, and Kingsley specifically mentioned a lack of milk. Their speech was " half articulate, nasal, guttural, made up almost entirely of vowels, like the speech of savages."

However, it is at least arguable that this low standard of living was a survival from an age-old past rather than a new-fangled horror. To some extent it was an expression of that way of life which was still evident in Northumberland, where as late as 1851 cows and pigs commonly slept under the same roof as the farm labourers ; and of the way of life in Western Scotland, where many farmers did not understand the principle of the rotation of crops, nor how to make hay for the winter, and where there still survived the system of communal occupancy with an annual exchange of plots—a system which gave little encouragement to anyone to improve his methods of cultivation.

The way in which the country districts suffered from the economic policy expressed in the repeal of the Corn Laws was that the general improvements manifest in the towns were less perceptible in the country. Agricultural wages fell as the prices of agricultural products fell. A good

†RATE OF WAGES AND PRICES IN THE EAST RIDING FOR THE YEARS, 1794-1850

	1794	1811	1850		
Farm servant with board	£10 *to* £13	£20 *to* £26	£14 *to* £16		
Day labourer without board, average of year	2s.	3s. 3d.	2s.		
				horse	
			hand	*power*	*steam*
Thrashing wheat per quarter	2s. 2d. to 3s. 4d.	5s. 6d. to 7s.	3s. 6d.	1s. 7½d.	7½d.
Reaping wheat per acre	6s. to 8s.	10s. to 11s. 6d.	7s. 6d.		
Wheat per bushel	5s. 9d.	9s. 6d.	5s. to 5s. 6d.		
Barley per bushel	4s. 1½d.	3s. 9d.	3s. 3d.		
Oats per bushel	2s. 6d.	2s. 9d.	2s.		
Beans per bushel	4s. 6d.	4s. 9d.	3s. 9d. to 4s.		
Wool per lb.	—	10d.	1s.		
Beef per lb.	3¼d.	7½d.	4½d.		
Mutton per lb.	4d.	8d.	4½d. to 5d.		
Butter per lb.	1s.	1s.	1s.		
Milk per quart	3d.	2d.	2d.		

† *Published in* The Times, *Jan. 3rd, 1851.*

wage for a day labourer on a farm in 1851 was 2s. a day and for a farm
servant £14 a year and board. Child labour could still be hired at such
extraordinary rates as 1s. a week, and "gang-makers," as they were
called, were still active in exploiting child labour for agriculture. Above
all other evidence that rural districts offered worse economic prospects
than urban ones was the fact that the drift from the countryside continued.

That there was poverty, and indeed abject poverty, a hundred years
ago in many parts of Britain, both in town and in country, is therefore
hardly to be disputed. Moreover, there was no systematic relief for what
a later generation of politicians came to call the "submerged tenth" of
the population. To offset these manifest deficiencies of the system, however, there were two factors of primary importance. These were the
extremely low cost of living and the opportunities both for enterprise
and for normal, conscientious labour, which occurred at all levels of
society. An examination of prices and wages will in fact show how easily,
perhaps how surprisingly easily, the necessities of life and quite a number
of luxuries could be bought, not only by those who owned some property,
but also by wage-earners who were not in sweated employment.

A working-class couple could begin married life without discomfort
in a furnished room at 4s. a week. Indeed the "model houses for the
labouring classes," which the Prince Consort caused to be erected opposite
the Great Exhibition, offered a sitting-room and kitchen combined, three
bedrooms, a scullery and a w.c. at an estimated weekly rental of 3s. 6d.
or 4s. each. *The Times* in 1851 carried advertisements of dwellings for
single men at 2s. 6d. a week, and at a lower level of living there was an
appreciable difference between the type of accommodation provided in
a lodging-house for 4d. a night and that provided for 3d.

Food and drink were correspondingly cheap. Herrings were sold at
three or four for 1d., oysters at four for 1d., soles at 1d. a pair, and even
salmon at 6d. a pound. The price of fish being what it was, it is not
surprising that it was a common gesture in a tavern to "stand fish round,"
fish and bread being provided at 1d. a head. Yet, in spite of the cheapness
of fish, the English were notorious for being meat-eaters, and rather low-
grade meat already cooked could be bought at 4d. a pound.

A cup of coffee, a drink which enjoyed a vogue even among the poorer
classes after the reduction of the duty in 1842, and two slices of bread

† HOUSEPAINTER'S EXPENDITURE

In 1845, per Week			In 1851, per Week		
	s.	*d.*		*s.*	*d.*
Rent	1	4	Rent	1	8
5 loaves	2	11	4 loaves	2	0
Butter	0	5	Butter	0	5
Tea	0	6	Tea	0	5
Meat (3 lbs.)	1	6	Meat (3 lbs.)	1	0
Potatoes	0	3	Potatoes	0	2
Beer (a pot)	0	4	Beer (a pint)	0	2
	7	3		5	10

† HOUSEPAINTER'S EARNINGS

	1845		1851	
	s.	*d.*	*s.*	*d.*
Earnings of 6 days	15	0		
Earnings of 3 days			7	6
Weekly income	15	0	7	6
Expenditure	7	3	5	10
Difference	7	9	1	8

† *These tables are based on personal investigations by Henry Mayhew and used by him in* London Life and the London Poor.

and butter could be bought at a coffee-stall in London for 1d. ; beer cost 1½d. a pint, and gin 1d. a glass. Fruit was also plentiful and cheap, oranges, for instance, costing no more in England than they did in Mediterranean countries. Grapes were sold in the London streets at 2d. a pound, and pears at eight for 1d. Just as food was cheap, so was fuel, and coal could be bought at 18s. a ton.

When one considers these prices, the conclusion seems inescapable that the workmen engaged on the construction of the Crystal Palace in Hyde Park, who staged a strike to press their claim for a payment of 5s. instead of 4s. a day, had the means of enjoying a very tolerable life. Moreover, these workmen were not in any sort of privileged position which enabled them to demand exceptionally good pay. There was a strike staged in 1851 by seamen in Hull, who objected to a proposal that wages should be reduced to 3s. a day. It is true that the strike was not only a protest against inadequate pay ; it was also a protest against various regulations sanctioned by the Board of Trade, which prescribed, among other penalties, the loss of a day's pay for such offences as using improper language, interrupting divine service by indecorous conduct, and washing clothes on Sundays. Nevertheless, even with 3s. a day the seamen could not have been altogether poverty-stricken.

Whatever advantages the working classes gained from the general cheapness of living were of course magnified in the lives of the middle classes, for the strenuous commercial competition of the time served to keep all prices low, the prices of luxuries as well as the prices of necessities.

The rent of what was probably fairly described as a " desirable residence " in the suburbs of London was £40 a year, and in Piccadilly an " unfurnished first floor," or, as it would now be called, a flat, was advertised in 1851 as to let at 31s. 6d. a week. A good suit of black clothes was made to measure for £3 10s. ; a private school would educate the sons of gentlemen for between £20 and £30 a year ; a first-class ticket from London to Paris via Calais cost £2 15s. ; a good piano cost 25 guineas ; and five-year-old vintage champagne cost £2 per dozen.

Such prices reveal more about the economic conditions of the middle classes at the beginning of the fifties than could be gained from a consideration of salaries alone. Figures for salaries tend to be misleading. It tells us little, for example, that a curate might earn some £70 a year,

the same salary as was offered in contemporary advertisements to " a
collector for a coal merchant " and a clerk-accountant " conversant with
mercantile business."   The reason why such information may be misleading is that the middle-class world of a hundred years ago was a world

---

SOUTH-EASTERN RAILWAY,

OPEN TO

READING, REIGATE, TUNBRIDGE WELLS, MAIDSTONE,
ASHFORD, RYE, HASTINGS, ST. LEONARD'S,
CANTERBURY, RAMSGATE, MARGATE, DEAL, FOLKESTONE,
AND DOVER.

SHORTEST ROUTE TO ALL PARTS OF THE CONTINENT.

LONDON TO PARIS DAILY IN 11 HOURS,

| To BRUSSELS in 12½, | To COLOGNE in 20, |
| To HAMBURGH in 43, | To BERLIN in 49. |

Sea Passage 1¾ Hours, Five Times a Day;

Twice by Folkestone and Boulogne, Three Times by Dover
and Calais.

TRAINS SEVEN TIMES A DAY
For FOLKESTONE and DOVER.

THROUGH FARES.

	1st Class.	2nd Class.	3rd Class.
London to Paris, via Boulogne	£2 10 6	£1 17 0	£1 7 6
London to Paris, via Calais	£2 15 0	£2 0 8	£1 10 2

*Return Tickets, available for 15 days, London to Paris and
back by special Express Trains :—*

| First Class . . . £4. | Second Class . . . £3. |

Trains every Hour to WOOLWICH, GRAVESEND,
and STROOD.

To GREENWICH every Quarter of an Hour.

SOUTH-EASTERN RAILWAY,   G. S. HERBERT, Sec.
London Bridge Terminus.   [135

Railway fares, 1851

of property, a world of capital in which those with social pretensions were not expected to live on their salaries.

Good salaries were indeed to be earned in the higher ranks of the professions. The Lord Chancellor's salary was £10,000 a year, and that of the Chief Justice of the Queen's Bench £8,000. In 1851, as a measure of economy, the annual allowance for the expenses of the British Ambassador in Paris was reduced from £10,000 to £8,000. Even more lucrative as a profession was the Church, and, according to the contemporary estimate of Joseph Hume, the income of the Archbishop of Canterbury was £19,182, that of the Bishop of Durham £19,066, and that of the Bishop of London £13,929.

In spite of the impressive evidence of these figures, it is nevertheless true that professional appointments were sought after, in many cases, not so much for the salary that was offered as for the social position that was conferred. The social desirability of even ill-paid Government posts was shown by the practice of openly advertising an offer of a " douceur," which might amount to as much as £2,000, to anyone who helped the advertiser to obtain a situation such as he wanted. This system was fairly widespread and served as a link in time between the age of unconcealed patronage and that of a solicitous Ministry of Labour.

Prosperity among the middle and upper classes was reckoned not in terms of salary but in terms of property, and property had attached to it a special kind of sanctity. The degree of this sanctity is not easily appreciated in the modern world, where 19s. 6d. may legitimately be deducted from £1 in the form of taxation, and where society provides other forms of protection besides a man's own possessions to safeguard him from the ultimate disaster. Those who were responsible for the dispensation of justice a hundred years ago, however, had no doubts about the sanctity of property. In the year 1851 a certain Andrew Caster, who described himself as " a poor Italian in great distress and as hungry as a wolf," was sentenced to six weeks' hard labour for stealing a pocket handkerchief. Yet in the same year James Wick, who kicked a woman to death, stated in his defence that she had tried to rob him ; the Court had no evidence except his own word of this attempted robbery, but the result was that he was convicted not of murder but of manslaughter, and was given only three months in prison.

To those who owned property at the time of the general expansion of trade, which occurred about the middle of the century, the accumulation of wealth came fairly easily. It was not even necessary to charge exorbitant rents or offer inadequate pay in order to prosper. The very lodging-houses which the humanitarian Shaftesbury established in Bloomsbury as models for the better treatment of the working classes brought in a steady six per cent annually, and a thirty-forty per cent annual return could be expected from the more disreputable lodging-houses.

Both shareholders and landowners did from time to time encounter difficulties. There was a financial crisis in 1848, which was largely caused by excessive gambling in railway shares. There was also a certain amount of genteel poverty. We find the ladies of Cranford practising " elegant economy " and accepting the convention that it was vulgar to offer substantial meals to guests. Those who entered honourable professions without adequate safeguards in the form of an independent income often had a hard time of it. In 1849 *The Times* revealed a case of an Army officer who had died of an epidemic in Barbados after seventeen years of service, and whose total emoluments over this period exceeded the sums he had to pay for his successive commissions by only £78.

It may also be said of those with social pretensions in the fifties that, with the general increase in prosperity, there was an increase in the expenditure considered necessary for keeping up appearances. Bigger houses, bigger families and a growing fondness for ornamentation in dress and in furniture all meant a larger outlay for the middle classes, and among the aristocracy, of course, there was still a tradition of largesse. However, nobody can reasonably complain at having to maintain a high level of expenditure, provided he has the means of doing so. The propertied classes a hundred years ago mostly had those means, and consequently they had few reasonable grounds for complaint. As the danger of revolution receded, they were less and less troubled by one anxiety which had understandably been felt by the wealthy in the first half of the century ; and, as far as the propertied classes were concerned, Emerson had good reason for stating as he did, when surveying the social scene about the middle of the century : " If there be one successful country in the universe for the last millenium, that country is England."

The view which any of us to-day may form on the merits or short-comings of the economic system in Britain a hundred years ago must depend on our individual political standpoints. If we believe, as most of us now do, in safeguards against the exploitation of the poorest and some form of security for all, then the system must be condemned. If, on the other hand, we believe simply in rewards which are commensurate with the personal success of the individual or of his forebears, then we must admit that the system succeeded.

There is, however, only a limited relevance in the application of the standards of a later age for judging the doings of an earlier one. If, instead, we apply to the time of the Great Exhibition those standards which most of its contemporaries considered applicable, we must con-clude that, as far as economic conditions were concerned, the new decade of the fifties opened in a flush of success, just as the decade of the forties had passed in an atmosphere of alarm in some quarters and of despair in others.

For the youthful in 1851, those whom Mr. Young suggests we might well envy, the prospects were certainly encouraging, and there is sig-nificance in the very prevalence of the expression, " to rise in life." The exceptionally ambitious and talented met no insurmountable obstacles, and there was a good deal of truth in the Duke of Argyll's assertion that even the aristocracy had no objection to accepting new men such as Disraeli. Rather less charitably, he commented that the only impediments in Disraeli's way were " not any want of external advantages, but his own often grotesque and unwarrantable opinions."

For the commercially minded the age was an ideal one, and for technicians all sorts of new careers were opening up as scientific advances were made. For the normal product of the universities—those who were better educated in the arts than in the sciences and to whom the rough-and-tumble of commerce made little appeal—the choice of a career was not difficult either : the Church was an expanding concern, the social standing it conferred was enviable, it satisfied most people intellectually, and it offered the most attractive emoluments to those who rose above its lower ranks.

As for the poor, their lot was still pitied by some humanitarians, but much less fervently than it had been ten years before. And for many of

Emigrant ships
Where other outlets failed, there remained the outlet of emigration

them, where other outlets failed, there remained the outlet of emigration, an outlet which the humanitarians, such as Shaftesbury, themselves encouraged. Emigration was often a hard remedy, but it was one which was widely accepted, so widely that in the three years immediately following the repeal of the Corn Laws about a quarter of a million people annually emigrated from Great Britain and Ireland. That the remedy was in many cases successful is shown by the standard of living which has long prevailed in countries such as Australia, New Zealand and Canada. Whatever else may be said for or against the economic system of a hundred years ago, it cannot be denied that the peopling of these countries was one of its most important and lasting by-products.

CHAPTER FOUR

THE HOME
Houses, Furniture, Clothes, Food

T HE popular picture of the Victorian, and especially the mid-Victorian, domestic scene which has been handed down to posterity is one of a closely knit family life, of which the basis was a strict form of monogamy and the expression an extreme form of prudery. There is a good deal of truth in this picture, but the truth is qualified by the fact that the picture was essentially that of the domestic life of the middle classes.

The morality which the world has come to describe as " Victorian " is, and must be, essentially a middle-class virtue. Like the elaborate ritual of primitive tribes, it is in its origin a form of protection against the upsurge of savagery. Victorian morality did not spring from the aristocrats, who instinctively felt themselves several generations removed from savagery ; it sprang from the middle classes, who were constantly at pains to emphasise the gulf which lay between themselves and the lower orders.

It has sometimes been suggested that one of the strongest influences in spreading the new standards of propriety and of domestic conduct was the example of the Royal Family. Certainly even the most ruthless investigators of the facts have failed to unearth any suggestion of scandal in the private lives of Queen Victoria and her Consort. There is no doubt that the way of life which prevailed at Court—the " damned morality," as Melbourne called it—influenced a certain circle. Palmerston once invaded the room of a lady who was a royal guest, and this misdemeanour was made the subject of a reproach years later in the course of one of his many political disputes with the Court. We have the testimony of Greville that the Queen was in the habit of freezing anyone who departed from rigid standards of etiquette. There is also some evidence that the Queen's expressed objection to the traditional custom of allowing gentlemen to remain for some hours over their wine, after the ladies had left the dining-room, had the effect of reducing after-dinner drunkenness.

However, the social and domestic habits of the Royal Family would not have been approved and imitated as in fact they were, if they had not appealed to feelings which were already current. In a more licentious age the conduct of the Queen and the cousin whom she married would have been regarded simply as an unusual departure—which indeed it was—from the traditional habits of a family not noted for its continence or its sobriety.

It is not surprising that posterity has come to accept the picture of middle-class domestic life of a hundred years ago as typical of all domestic life of the period. Not only were the middle classes rapidly expanding in numbers both by natural increase and the accession of new members. Their social influence grew correspondingly. In the political field, their power had become such that Cobden even tried to persuade Peel to become the leader of a new middle-class party ; and in the field of education it was significant that Lord Ashley, himself a hereditary peer and an Old Harrovian, expressed his approval of upper-middle-class standards by sending his son to Rugby, because as he expressed it, there was a need for " deeper, sterner stuff ; less of refinement and more of truth." Also —perhaps most important of all as far as the picture handed down to posterity is concerned—the middle classes were writing the great majority of the novels. As many of the best novelists were women, some picture of mid-Victorian middle-class domestic life is familiar to-day to almost every literate Englishman.

Nevertheless, there were other domestic patterns in England a hundred years ago beside the middle-class pattern with which we have become familiar. Much of the traditional aristocratic manner of living was retained, including something of that eighteenth-century magnificence which Thackeray suggested had been almost Augustan. In one of Disraeli's later novels an impressive picture is given which was no doubt

based on the author's personal experiences. When Lothair returned
home, " the house steward, the chief butler, the head gardener, the chief
of the kitchen, the head keeper, the head forester, and grooms of the
stud and of the chambers, formed one group behind the housekeeper . . .
half a dozen powdered gentlemen, glowing in crimson liveries, indicated
the presence of my Lord's footmen, while the rest of the household, considerable in numbers, were arranged in groups according to their own
sex, and at a respectful distance."

This picture was not one of Disraeli's essays in fantasy. By 1851
there was rather less magnificence than there had been a quarter of a
century earlier, in the hey-day of the first Earl of Durham, who had once
stated that a man could jog along on £70,000 a year. However, when
the Queen visited the Duke of Buckingham in 1845, her carriage was met
by five hundred of the Duke's tenants on horseback, and six hundred
more tenants, dressed in smocks, lined the avenue of her approach.
A number of noble households were still largely self-contained com-
munities, and the occupational census of 1851 showed agriculture as the
only industry which exceeded domestic service in the number of people
to whom it gave employment : 1,790,000 were listed as employed in
agriculture, and 1,039,000 in domestic service. The domestic servants,
in fact, numbered nearly twice as many as the cotton workers and more
than four times as many as the coal miners, although it is true that many
of these servants were employed in relatively modest middle-class households.

The aristocracy was far from eliminated a hundred years ago as the
ruling class of a feudal society. It was still regarded as the class from
which those who held the highest Government posts were normally to
be recruited. Palmerston had the ideal background for a political career
as the holder of an Irish peerage. This clearly indicated his aristocratic
birth, yet allowed him to sit in the House of Commons. Towards the
end of his life the Duke of Argyll could declare : " I speak of the House
of Commons simply as an assembly of men, which it is of importance for
every politician to belong to, even for a time, however short, that he may
know its members as widely as he can."

The lives of many big landowners were still largely predetermined by
the responsibilities of running vast estates, and the majority of them

retained that preference for country to town life, which has long char-
acterised the English upper class, and which is revealed in the significance
attached to the very terms, " county families " and " bourgeoisie."

Nevertheless, in their social and domestic habits the aristocracy were
drawing steadily nearer to an upper-middle class, so that to a foreigner,
even an observant one such as Emerson, the two were hardly distinguish-
able. The number of people who, in Emerson's estimate, were coming
and going in London to make up high society was 70,000, far too large
a number to admit of only the aristocracy.

A reflection of the acceptance of middle-class standards of decorum
by the aristocracy can be seen, for instance, in the lives of successive
Dukes of Devonshire. The sixth Duke of Devonshire, whose patronage
allowed Paxton, the creator of the Crystal Palace, to follow his remarkable
career, was the son of a famous beauty. This was the Duchess Georgiana,
who had been painted by both Reynolds and Gainsborough. The sixth
Duke's father had lived concurrently with the Duchess Georgiana and
with Lady Elizabeth Foster, having children by both of them, while the
two women remained close friends. The sixth Duke in his turn lived for
some ten years with a certain Elizabeth Warwick, but he did it discreetly,
and she was not flaunted in society ; moreover, the sixth Duke was a
bachelor. By the middle of the last century Elizabeth Warwicks had not
disappeared from ducal households, but they were becoming much rarer ;
Elizabeth Fosters and Georgianas were creatures of a bygone age.

The task of inculcating a proper decorum into the sexual and domestic
habits of the lower orders was in many respects a more formidable one
than that of modifying the ways of the aristocracy. Certainly, according
to middle-class standards, there was plenty of room for improvement in
working-class morals. Mayhew, who approached the subject in a more
objective and analytical manner than other contemporary observers,
estimated that among London costermongers only one couple out of
ten who were living together were legally married. Cohabitation commonly
began at the age of fourteen, and the marriage ceremony was widely
regarded as a waste of money. Some hint of the extent of prostitution
has already been given, and it seems to have been no rarity for this way
of life to be entered upon at the age of twelve.

Alcoholism was also a powerful influence in undermining domesticity.

Georgiana Spencer, Duchess of Devonshire, by Sir Joshua Reynolds

The common custom of choosing Saturday night in a pub as the time and place for paying workmen their wages naturally disrupted the domestic life of the men, yet an estimate dating from the forties suggested that 60 per cent of the frequenters of pubs were women. Crimes of a domestic nature were also not uncommon, a circumstance which led the *Spectator* to declare that " among Englishwomen of the humbler classes the settlement of conjugal or pecuniary difficulties by the summary help of arsenic is already a habit, and one that is increasing."

There were perhaps three main ways in which the domestic habits of the working classes were directly influenced by the more exacting middle classes. One was the missionary approach ; the second was by the setting of an example which it paid to imitate ; the third was by continuous personal contact.

The missionary approach took both an ecclesiastical and an educational form. It was expressed not only in sabbatarianism and temperance reform ; it was also seen in such aspects of the Evangelical revival as the Ragged School movement. There was still a social stratum below which the Established Church, with its pews for the rich and what Ashley called " nooks and corners reserved for the working class," did not penetrate. In this sub-stratum only the Irish, who were in contact with a few scattered Roman Catholic priests, knew much of religion. On the other hand, Ragged Schools were established in districts into which even the police would not venture unless they were armed and in considerable numbers. Although many mothers first welcomed Ragged Schools simply as a means of disposing of children during the daytime, the ultimate influence of these institutions was incalculable. In the domestic sphere, however, it was an influence which was inevitably slow and almost imperceptible.

A more immediate method of making an impression was that of setting an example of respectability. The urge to be considered respectable is one which is never wholly eliminated from any section of a community, and, perhaps not surprisingly, it was to be found even in the London slums of a hundred years ago. Mayhew, for instance, tells a story of a girl, whom even he classified as belonging to the " very poor," and who was giving birth to a child on a bundle of straw. Her family paid nine-pence a week for the apartment, and she had beside her a clean nightcap for use, as she put it, " against the doctor came." The feeling revealed

Lady Elizabeth Foster. The sixth Duke of Devonshire's father lived concurrently with the Duchess Georgiana and with Lady Elizabeth Foster

in this incident was certainly susceptible to influence by those who were comparatively well-to-do. In an age in which the middle classes were steadily recruiting new members from those who had formerly been socially beneath them, and in which the poor had much to gain by rising in the social scale, the spread of respectability was naturally precipitated.

Continuous direct contact between the middle classes and persons whom they regarded as being of a lower order was chiefly maintained through the system of domestic service. The employment of some domestic help was both socially *de rigueur* and economically feasible even in the most modest middle-class families. When Dora and David Copperfield set up home in a tiny cottage, Copperfield commented : " We had a servant, of course. She kept house for us." At a time when £10 a year plus board was considered a good wage for a servant, this assumption of the necessity of employing domestic help is not surprising.

The structure of middle-class houses was in itself a cogent reason for relying on a considerable number of servants. Bathrooms with a direct hot and cold water supply were still a rarity, and hot water had normally to be carried. Food, as a contemporary expression which was rich in meaning indicated, was also " sent up " from the kitchen. Moreover, the mistress of a middle-class household was not expected to simplify the tasks of the servants by rendering any direct assistance. As a clergyman's wife who wrote to *The Times* in 1851 declared—without, it may be noted, a suggestion of reproach—" few mistresses pretending to ' gentility ' ever venture into the kitchen."

Much indeed was demanded of servants for their £10 a year plus board, and something of the conditions in which they were expected to live is still revealed in the servants' rooms of mid-Victorian houses. However, whether they liked it or not, they were regarded as being in contact with their betters, and for that very reason they had to regulate their conduct. A servant girl might, for instance, escape from a mistress who beat her and take to the streets ; but as long as she remained in service she was bound to behave in a manner which was considered respectable.

By a variety of means, therefore, a standard of propriety which was characteristically middle-class was gaining wider and wider acceptance in Britain a hundred years ago, and the extent to which it spread is still revealed in certain aspects of present-day society. In that movement lies the main justification for regarding the middle-class domestic scene as the typical domestic scene of the age.

Apart from its extreme propriety, the outstanding characteristic of English middle-class domestic life a hundred years ago was a peculiar blend of comfort and ostentation, both of them qualities which can generally be purchased with money. This characteristic blend was revealed even in the food which was eaten. On the whole this food was plentiful and good. Emerson noted particularly among the praiseworthy qualities of English life the exceptional personal liberty, the plentiful supply of food, and the excellence of the ale and mutton. In illustration of his thesis he maintained that the average Englishman was slightly larger than the average American, although the English had a tendency to grow too fat. The popular English conception of a Frenchman was of a creature who was emaciated and half-starved.

English inns at that time had an international reputation for their comfort and appointments, and the English were well known for being exacting in the matter of food. Certainly the meals which were prepared in the more prosperous English homes accustomed them to a high standard. A breakfast such as Trollope described has an entrancing ring to-day. " There was tea and coffee, dry toast and buttered toast, muffins, hot bread and cold bread, white bread and brown bread, eggs in napkins, and crispy bits of bacon under silver covers. There were little fishes in a little box, and devilled kidneys frizzling on a hot-water dish, and standing on the sideboard a huge ham and a huge sirloin." Venison, quails, pheasants and larks were dishes which a country gentleman might expect to see on his table any day ; grapes and pineapples were commonly grown in hothouses ; and the English were still, in the absence of prohibitive customs duties, a nation of wine-drinkers.

Like the etiquette book, the cookery book enjoyed a considerable vogue a hundred years ago. Mrs. Beeton's masterpiece had not yet burst upon the world, but the more prosperous middle classes were continually receiving instructions on the type of meal which the well-bred guest could expect. In 1851 Charles Dickens's wife published a cookery book under the significant *nom de plume* of Lady Maria Clutterbuck. A typical menu which she proposed for a dinner at which there would be six to ten persons offered carrot soup, turbot with shrimp sauce, lobster patties, stewed kidneys, roast saddle of lamb, boiled turkey, knuckle of ham, mashed and brown potatoes, stewed onions, cabinet pudding, blancmange and cream, and macaroni.

For all its general excellence, there was a tendency to excess in the diet of the well-to-do, an excess which was in itself a form of ostentation. When Jorrocks dined with the Muleygrubs he was offered pea-soup or mutton-broth, skate or haddock, beef and boiled turnips, a degenerate turkey, reindeer tongue, sausages, minced veal, rissoles, stewed celery, pigs' feet, game-pie, black puddings, partridges and snipe. The meal was portrayed by Surtees as a horrifying one, and by the time he had come to the end of the courses described all that Jorrocks could take was breath. However, the Muleygrubs were not uncommon beings a hundred years ago.

In the furnishing of the houses of the well-to-do the same combination of comfort and ostentation was evident. Much of the furniture has a solidity which, after a period of revulsion, is to-day quite widely appreciated. Craftsmanship was still far from being the obsolescent skill it is now. It is significant that the authors of *The History of Everyday Things* chose the year 1851 as the dividing point in time between the making of items of furniture which can now be cherished as antiques, and the making of those which are described simply as second-hand. Examples of the best furniture of the time are still retained in some of the London clubs which were then being built,

Chair in papier mâché

and the chairs in such cases are usually solid, comfortable, sleep-inducing containers.

Deviations did, however, occur in the furniture design of a hundred years ago from the primary object of providing comfort, and these deviations tended to become more and more frequent. The results took the form of attempts to combine the massive and the frivolous, so that the death-pangs of rococo came to be expressed in materials as inappropriate as mahogany. The solid was continually merging into the ornate, as the show-pieces displayed at the Great Exhibition revealed only too clearly. *Papier mâché* and gilt stucco were in common use ; wallpapers competed with one another in the harshness of their colours ; utilitarian objects, such as sideboards, pianos and bookcases, were elaborately ornamented ; the introduction of oriental themes in a style which was later to reach its apogee in the Albert Memorial was beginning to be popular ; and continually appearing, whether in woodwork or in china, was that peculiar Victorian treatment of the female nude, the treatment accorded by Powers in his much admired statue of the Greek slave, and by Winterhalter in his less inhibited paintings. This treatment no doubt satisfied the demand which to-day is largely met by the sun-bathing magazines, but it was somewhat deficient in artistic inspiration.

The houses of the middle classes revealed many of the same qualities as their furniture. Better fittings provided a greater degree of comfort than had been known in earlier ages. There was a steady improvement in plumbing, and the general use of gas lighting allowed greater inroads to be made into the hours of darkness for social purposes. The family dinner, for which dressing was *de rigueur* among the well-to-do, commonly took place at 6 p.m., but when guests were invited it might well begin some two hours later. The dinner would last an hour or perhaps even two hours before the ladies left the room, and the gentlemen might then spend another hour over their wine.

There was also plenty of solid, sensible domestic architecture. The neo-classical was as much in vogue as the neo-gothic, in spite of the strenuous activities of Sir George Gilbert Scott in gothicising English churches, and in spite of the evident neo-gothic qualities in Barry's highly successful Houses of Parliament, which were formally opened, though still incomplete, in 1852. Post-Ruskin gothicism and the red, yellow and blue brick of Butterfield had not yet left the mark they were later to leave on English towns.

That popular Victorian treatment of the female nude accorded by Powers in his much admired statue of the Greek slave

Nevertheless, in domestic architecture, as in furniture, ornateness was as much in demand as was comfort, and it was available in forms which would hardly have been conceivable in earlier ages. The very demand for houses which the growth of the population and the growth of prosperity created meant that more and more builders and more and more architects were employed. The effect of this was not only a lowering of standards, but also a breakdown of the disciplines which architects' offices had formerly imposed on newcomers to the profession. Extravagance easily became a substitute for order ; the age had no one style of its own ; and refuge was sought in the evocation and imitation, with varying degrees of success, of almost every style which English architects had created in the past. The model of a Tudor house shown at the Great Exhibition serves as a vivid reminder of what imitation executed in the spirit of ostentation can bring about.

Naturally enough, those outstanding characteristics of the middle classes which their home life revealed were also reflected in different forms in contemporary fashions in dress. In women's clothes prudery especially and, to a lesser extent, the ostentatious display of wealth governed the taste of the time.

The revelations of the female form which the vogues of twenty or thirty years earlier had allowed were banned by the middle of the century. Instead, maximum concealment of the body was aimed at, to which end even devices such as the wearing of bonnets and of gloves indoors were employed. Garments of underclothing became steadily more numerous. The quantity of underclothing which Dr. Cunnington lists as being fashionable in the forties was a chemise reaching down to the knees, some half a dozen petticoats, drawers, stays and, as a novelty, the camisole or " waistcoat." Drawers, a nineteenth-century innovation, were, he maintains, still largely an upper-class garment before the sixties. The downward lacing of stays had the effect of flattening breasts, and ballroom dresses of the period, though they did leave the shoulders bare, commonly ended in a straight line above the bosom. This served to eliminate, as far as possible, any impression of its shape.

It would be difficult to maintain that even the more elaborate fashions of the time served to enhance the beauty of the female body. Of the institutional costume imposed on certain young women of gentility, the observations of Jane Eyre provide a discouraging impression : " Plain locks combed from their faces, not a curl visible ; in brown dresses, made high and surrounded by a narrow tucker about the throat . . . ; all too wearing woollen stockings and country-made shoes, fastened with brass buckles. Above twenty of them clad in this costume, were full-grown girls, or rather young women ; it suited them ill, and gave an air of oddity even to the prettiest."

Though prudery was expressed in every aspect of women's dress of the time, fashion was nevertheless studied and sought after as eagerly as at any time before or since. Elaborate care was taken to achieve the proper compromise between the " fast " and the " dowdy," as the two undesirable extremes were called, and to be fashionable became a steadily more expensive accomplishment as the prosperity of the middle classes increased. Not only did the very number of garments worn before the general acceptance of the artificial crinoline demand a considerable outlay; the popularity of silks and satins, of velvet and lace, and the steady increase in the quantity of jewellery worn, all served to make poverty and fashion steadily more incompatible.

Comfort, the third outstanding characteristic of middle-class domesticity noted, was little evident in women's clothes. However, comfort was in many respects the prerogative of the male. In men's fashions there was a concurrent trend towards a greater degree of comfort and towards that sobriety or sombreness which has prevailed in masculine dress from that day to this. Tight-waisted frock-coats, elaborate waist-coats and high tall-hats had not disappeared. However, black was more and more widely worn ; the cravat was beginning to be abandoned in favour of the narrow necktie ; and concessions to comfort were increasingly made in the form of smoking-caps and smoking-jackets.

Women's clothing was not only uncomfortable, it was positively inconvenient ; and it was an expression and, to a minor extent, a cause of the restricted life which the well-bred female was obliged to lead. The use of back fasteners and hooks on dresses shows how dependent ladies were on the services of their maids or other members of their family, and the wearing of half a dozen petticoats did not encourage violent or sustained movement.

Posterity has come to imagine the domestic life of the young lady of a hundred years ago as one which was spent almost exclusively indoors, and in which the principal distraction was either embroidery or speculation about the possibilities of receiving a proposal of marriage. The picture is of course an exaggerated one. Railway travel, for instance, was opening up many new opportunities for social intercourse, not only

Fashions for April, 1851

in the form of visits to friends but also in popularising holidays by the seaside. Nevertheless, the social and domestic life of young ladies was indeed hedged round by conventions which in many cases served to reduce it to an appalling emptiness.

The etiquette books of the Victorian age are well-known curios to-day, and dissertations on what did and what did not constitute ladylike conduct have caused endless amusement to readers of the twentieth century. What, however, is less considered by posterity is the utter vacuity which those conventions imposed. Calling hours at Cranford, for instance, were between twelve and three, and calls were not expected to last more than a quarter of an hour, a period within which it must have been difficult to discuss anything of interest. The habit of suppressing feeling was also becoming ingrained in the English, and Emerson noted that no enthusiasm was permitted by good taste except at the opera.

Moreover, the choice of society was closely controlled by considerations of caste : the curate, who in a later age was to be considered only half a man, was then widely regarded as the most desirable suitor for the well-bred young woman. In Peacock's Reverend Mr. Larynx a picture had been painted of the intermediary species between the socially minded clergyman of the old age and the socially minded clergyman of the new. " Nothing came amiss to him—a game at billiards, at chess, at draughts, at backgammon, at piquet, or at all-fours in a *tête-à-tête* " ; he would " crack jokes " with Mr. Hilary, but he would also " hand Mrs. Hilary to the piano, take charge of her fan and her gloves, and turn over her music with surprising dexterity." The curate of 1851 was more dexterous at turning over music than at playing backgammon.

The well-bred young lady of a hundred years ago was indeed a protected creature. She was protected from vice, protected from danger, protected even from serious work. She was expected to marry young, with her parents' consent but not altogether at her parents' prompting. This convention served to retain the possibilities of romance, while eliminating most of the more obvious romantic dangers. It was, however, from the very vigilance with which the whole system of protection was applied that the movement arose which, more than any other one cause, was eventually to destroy the domestic structure of the mid-Victorian world.

BLOOMERISM—AN AMERICAN CUSTOM.

*Mrs. Bloomer, an American, whose name gave a new word to the
English language, made a lecture tour of England*

Two events occurred within the space of a few years which, though of
little immediate importance in themselves, were indicative of future
trends. In 1851 Mrs. Bloomer, an American, whose name gave a new
word to the English language, made a lecture tour of England in which
she advocated the wearing by women of a garment then known as
"pantaloons." In 1849 Bedford College for Women was founded. It
was to serve, in the words of the founder, as "a place where by the
culture of the mind and the acquiring of some knowledge young women
might be saved from the dreary futility of the life led by the greater number
of those whose parents belonged to the professional and upper middle
classes." Mrs. Bloomer was regarded chiefly as a suitable subject for the
cartoonists, and Bedford College, where chaperons were required for

young ladies even when they attended lectures by male professors, soon encountered financial difficulties.

The emancipation of women was still, in short, a groping movement. Mary Ann Evans, who in 1851 became assistant editor of the *Westminster Review*, still found it prudent to follow the example of the Brontës in publishing her works under such a masculine pseudonym as that of George Eliot. Nevertheless, the movement was already launched, and the more it gathered strength, the more it hastened the collapse of the whole structure of middle-class domestic life which was in being around 1851.

The middle classes, aiming at purity, condemned their young women to a life of emptiness. In time that void was found to be intolerable, and the way in which it was filled not only modified the existing domestic structure ; in the end it caused its complete destruction. In that fact lay the proof of the failure of the system. Whatever desirable features the system may have had—and it had a considerable number—it proved to be unworkable, and it was the movement towards the emancipation of women, with all that it involved in education and in taste, in the economic life of the community and in the readjustment of sexual relations, which was the most irresistible and crushing cause of its collapse.

CHAPTER FIVE

ENTERTAINMENT

Theatre, Music, Sport

ONE of the factors most strongly differentiating the present century from preceding ones is the immense hold which the entertainment industry now has upon our lives. Not only have we entirely new forms of entertainment of tremendous social importance, such as the radio, films and television, but most of the older forms of entertainment which survive have had applied to them a revolutionary technique of distribution and popularisation. To that extent our lives, which may or may not be the better, are unquestionably the richer.

A hundred years ago the provision of mass entertainment was, by comparison with modern standards, scanty. However, the desire for such entertainment was widespread, and when it was offered it was usually accepted with eagerness. In 1851, for instance, the public execution of Henry Groom at Norwich was carried out before what the newspapers of the day called " an immense concourse of persons." This popular hunger was equally evident in the case of spectacles of a more edifying nature. Two years earlier the last stages in the erection of the tubular bridge over the Menai Straits had been watched, so contemporary observers asserted, by tens of thousands of spectators.

The event which perhaps provided the clearest proof of the popular need was the Great Exhibition. During the period of about six months in which it remained open, the Exhibition was visited by more than six million people—and this in spite of the fact that the charge for admission was never reduced below one shilling. On the shilling admission days the number of visitors sometimes exceeded a hundred thousand. The Exhibition had in fact a success without parallel in the history of spectacles of its kind, and contemporary opinion was almost unanimous in considering it the outstanding event of the year in England. That this was so can perhaps be more convincingly explained by the generally unsatisfied demand for mass entertainment than in any other way.

There were of course many kinds of entertainment offered to the British public a hundred years ago, but most of them were the traditional kinds which had been available in some form for centuries. The distribution of entertainment remained haphazard, and, unlike the basic industries, the entertainment industry was not modernised to meet the demands of a new society.

In the construction of theatres, for instance, the period around the middle of the century was one of stagnation. No new theatres were built in London between 1845 and 1866, and little theatre building was done in the provinces.

The art of the dramatist had also fallen to an extremely low level, and not a single play of the time survives to-day except as a piece for the collectors of the more curious Victoriana. Comedies, poetic dramas and melodramas were all produced in large numbers, but with a sorry lack of either originality or inspiration. Comedy, for the most part, was an affair of stock figures—comic Irishmen, comic rustics and comic fops. In the poetic drama a debased Shakespearian tradition survived, and there was a riot of the worst elements of romanticism. Only in melodrama was any sort of realism widely accepted as a form of presentation.

The type of drama which the playgoer in 1851 might choose to see was, for instance, a moral piece entitled *Good for Nothing*. This was produced with success at the Haymarket. The central figure was an orphan girl, who was brought up by two foster-fathers, one a market gardener and the other a railway stoker. The stoker was of uncouth appearance and could not read, but was skilled with his fists. A young carpenter aroused the girl's love, and she was fortunate enough to be given £5 by the parents of a child she had saved from drowning. With this and the contents of a money-box, which her foster-parents had not touched, she was able to marry the carpenter and pension off the foster-parents.

Another representative piece produced in 1851 was a farce called *Cool as a Cucumber*. In this an adventurer picked up a cigar-case belonging to a gentleman's son and thus gained admission to the gentleman's house. The son had been banished from his home because of a *mésalliance*, but the adventurer, after various mix-ups, in which the son was treated as a burglar, effected a family reconciliation. As alternatives to such pieces the playgoer was offered, for example, the colourful works of Dion Boucicault. Four of Boucicault's plays were produced in 1851, and their titles were indicative of their contents : *Sixtus V, or the Broken Vow* ; *Love in a Maze* ; *The Queen of Spades, or the Gambler's Secret* ; *O'Flannigan and the Fairies*.

Quality was not readily found in the theatrical productions of the time, but there was certainly no lack of quantity. Double or triple bills provided shows lasting from 6.30 until after midnight, and theatrical companies often numbered more than a hundred persons.

The nature of theatrical productions was still influenced by the curious legal monopoly which had remained in force until 1843. This monopoly had meant that legitimate drama could be performed only at Drury Lane, Covent Garden and, in the summer months, the Haymarket. These theatres with a legitimate tradition were all inordinately large ones, and that fact alone had a powerful influence on the type of dramatic presentation which was still in fashion eight years after the monopoly had ended.

Acting in large theatres calls for broad rather than subtle effects, for declamation and the extravagant gesture rather than for the technique of realism. Moreover, there were other factors apart from the size of theatres which helped to keep the old traditions of acting alive. Lighting was still crude, in contrast with the improvements which had been introduced into the French theatres ; bright lights were commonly shown in the auditorium, and the faces of actors were disfigured by reflections from the footlights. Orchestra stalls, which brought critics of greater refinement to the front rows, though an innovation of the eighteen-twenties, were accepted only slowly and with some reluctance in the forties. The chief arbiters of taste were still the comparatively uninhibited occupants of the pits, who occupied the whole of the floor of the auditorium.

For these reasons the actors of the time had to contend with many of the difficulties which the actors in silent films later encountered.

Gestures had to be unmistakable, and meanings of situations were commonly made so clear that they could be understood even without the assistance of the spoken word. Consequently, the technique of the actors of a hundred years ago was such as would appear crude to modern audiences, just as the technique of the silent screen actors often appears crude to modern film-goers.

Like the silent films, the large theatres of a hundred years ago tended to offer extravagance of spectacle rather than subtlety of situation. This extravagance had a considerable appeal in an age in which there was a general delight in the use of new mechanical devices and in the display of wealth. A popular production of *The Tempest* in 1852 began, for instance, with the shipwrecked vessel rolling in the sea and showing first one of her sides and then the other to the audience. Other common devices used to magnify the splendour of the settings were gauze to indicate mists, waterfalls for Scottish Highland scenery, and dioramas to display the wonders of the East. Where other attractions failed, it was a popular device to allow horses to be ridden on to the stage.

Nevertheless, the first signs of the new realism, which was to grow in strength in the second half of the century with the advent of Robertson and the Bancrofts, and which was to effect one of the greatest revolutions in the history of the English theatre, were beginning by 1851 to be apparent.

The great Macready, who made his last stage appearance in that year in the part of Macbeth, had already instituted lasting reforms. His habit of rehearsing parts with the same intensity as he showed when facing an audience had proved contagious ; he had demonstrated how effectively the whisper and the unexpected emphasis on familiar words could be employed ; and he had done much to ensure that correct Shakespearian texts were used.

During the later years of Macready's reign Charles Kean, himself rather a moderate actor who was handicapped by a poor voice and a lisp, was beginning to make realistic, everyday interior sets acceptable to audiences ; and during his period of management at the Princess's Theatre he insisted on a more or less uniform standard of acting throughout his casts. He also proved in a manner which had not been demonstrated before that the long run could be financially successful.

The great Macready made his last stage appearance in 1851 in the part of Macbeth

Perhaps even more revolutionary in its effects than the work of Macready or Kean was, as Professor Watson has convincingly shown, the Vestris-Mathews partnership at Covent Garden and later at the Lyceum. Madame Vestris was an Italian singer, who had been brought up in France and had married her leading actor, Charles Mathews. She gained her early experience of theatrical management at the small Olympic Theatre in London at a time when the monopoly of legitimate drama was still in force. Being forbidden by law to stage legitimate drama, the Olympic had to rely on what were known as burlettas, an ill-defined term, the general implication of which was that the show must contain a certain amount of music and consist of three instead of five acts. It proved possible to evade the law relating to music by having a tinkling piano providing a running and inoffensive accompaniment ; there was no reason, as posterity has since realised, why a serious play should not be produced in three acts ; and in a small theatre the Vestris-Mathews players showed how effects could be achieved by talking to each other rather than almost exclusively to the audiences. G. H. Lewes summarised their technique significantly when he described it as " well-bred."

Another factor which helped to improve the general status of the theatre was the interest shown by the Royal Family. In the immediate past the theatre had lacked the patronage it needed. It was despised by the majority of intellectuals ; it differed from the theatres in many other countries in that it was not supported by the State ; it had on the whole failed to attract the aristocracy ; and it was widely condemned by clergymen as an immoral institution. In view of the amount of soliciting by prostitutes which took place in the auditorium, this was not surprising. The interest shown by the Queen and Prince Albert and the consequent appointment of Charles Kean in 1849 as manager of the Windsor Castle theatricals therefore gave the stage a new and much needed respectability.

The revolution in the English theatre had not been effected by 1851. The profession of dramatist was not regarded as an exalted one, nor was it well rewarded. Professional dramatists such as Planché and Fitzball were turning out half a dozen plays a year and were lucky if they made £50 to £100 from any of them. This was at a time when Dickens was building up that fortune which enabled him, in spite of generous expenditure and large family commitments, ultimately to leave nearly £100,000 ;

and when Tennyson, after the publication of *In Memoriam*, found that the sales of his poems would justify him in getting married. Yet there was already an indication of what was to come in the theatre in the fact that in 1851 Thomas William Robertson, the author of *Caste* and the great pioneer figure in the new English theatrical realism, had his first play produced.

There was one kind of theatrical performance which enjoyed considerable prestige in the middle of the century and in which there was, perhaps for that very reason, a generally high standard of performance. This was the opera. Benjamin Lumley, the director of Her Majesty's Theatre at the time of the Great Exhibition, declared in his reminiscences that the period of his control was " the most brilliant period of the history of Italian opera in the British Isles." He had no hesitation in styling Her Majesty's " the first theatre in the kingdom—may it not be added the first in Europe ? " Lumley, it is true, was a man who apparently regretted nothing he ever did, and he was just as proud of having fired Lola Montez as of having engaged Jenny Lind and Madame Sontag. Nevertheless, Her Majesty's Theatre under his direction had indeed a claim to the description of " brilliance." The habitués were much more refined than those who went to witness straight plays ; the theatre was known as an international centre of fashion ; and such was the success of Jenny Lind during her short career in England that it became a commonplace among newspaper reporters, when describing the crowds of the fashionable who assembled at the Great Exhibition, to compare them with those who attended a Jenny Lind first night. It was rumoured that Jenny Lind was offered £25,000 for a five-month engagement at Her Majesty's, and the *Musical Times* gruffly suggested that she should " make hay while the sun shines ; public lunacy is generally of short duration."

Opera a hundred years ago in England meant primarily Italian opera. There was indeed something of a revival of native opera, of which the highlight was Balfe's *Bohemian Girl*, which was first produced in 1843; but the accepted convention from which it would have been financially dangerous for managers to depart, was that opera was primarily an Italian product. Even when Beethoven's *Fidelio* was produced in London in 1851, the rendering was an Italian translation from the German.

JENNY LIND'S LAST NIGHT IN ENGLAND,"

It was rumoured that Jenny Lind was offered £25,000
for a five-month engagement at Her Majesty's

As an interlude between the acts of operas it was a common practice to stage a ballet, and the ballet was regarded by some managers as the part of the performance most certain to draw the audiences. The emphasis in the production of ballet was generally on spectacle and gymnastics.

The emphasis in the production of ballet was generally on spectacle and gymnastics

A growing tendency towards greater realism was evident in some of the sets, but the dramatic form of dancing which the Russians were later to introduce was still virtually unknown. Carlyle was not a ballet fan, but there may have been some truth in his description of a visit to Her Majesty's Theatre in 1851, in which he wrote of girls " spinning there in strange, mad vortexes, and then suddenly fixing themselves motionless, each upon her left or right great toe with the other leg stretched out at an angle of ninety degrees . . . a motion peculiar to the opera—perhaps the ugliest, and certainly one of the most difficult, ever taught a female creature."

The musical entertainment provided outside the theatres was such as would seem intolerably meagre to the modern public. The regular provision of concerts of quality was still practically the monopoly of the Philharmonic Society, which in 1846 decided to appoint a regular conductor for the first time. The society's choice was Sir Michael Costa, but at the end of his tenure of office it was thought preferable to have a conductor with an international reputation. The candidate selected was Richard Wagner, but the experiment was not regarded as a success either by the orchestra or by the conductor, Wagner basing his objections, not unreasonably, on the low standard of orchestral playing.

Periodic festivals brought a certain amount of music to the provinces for a few days at a time. The Three Choirs Festival was a popular event, and it was at the Birmingham Musical Festival that Mendelssohn's *Elijah* was first given to the world. The comment of the *Musical Times* was that it was " but imperfectly given, from the want of proper rehearsals."

Promenade concerts were organised by Balfe with some success, and in 1849 Sterndale Bennett, who was later to succeed Wagner as the Philharmonic's conductor, founded the Bach Society. For the masses, however, little was done to provide music of any quality. An experiment was made in Liverpool in giving good concerts at a price deliberately fixed to attract the working classes, and attendances were large. In London, however, the poor were more likely to drift towards the penny gaff, a performance of bawdy dancing and singing which took place on a stage some eight feet square with, as a rule, gas jets on either side of the stage, on which the audience might light their pipes.

Sport as an entertainment for the masses also played a much smaller part in the life of the community than it does to-day, and the interest of partisans was not kept constantly roused by reports in popular newspapers. The only sports of which any accounts appeared in *The Times* of 1851 were horse-racing, hunting, coursing, cricket and rowing. Such meagre reports as were published were tucked away in a corner under the not very sensational heading, " Sporting Intelligence."

A hundred years ago there was a much closer connection between most of the sport which was practised and animal life than there is to-day. Now, although there may be an individual interest in hunting, shooting or fishing, the only animal sports which arouse general excitement are horse-racing and greyhound-racing. In the middle of the last century, however, cock-fighting had only just become illegal, and its popularity died hard. Bear and bull baiting, which had been prohibited earlier, were also still indulged in surreptitiously. In London cruel dog-fights, from which the police were excluded, were regularly organised, and in the country there still survived various sports of great antiquity which are now unknown. Miss Christina Hole, for instance, recently reproduced an authenticated record of a remarkable foot-racing contest which took

The start of the 1851 Derby

place on the Yorkshire moors in 1851. This was the traditional contest for the prize of the bride's garter on the occasion of a wedding. The participants were the young men of the district, who had to run stark naked from the church to the bride's home.

Horse-racing has for centuries enjoyed in England both the prestige of distinguished patronage and the popularity of the masses. A hundred years ago it was the common practice for the House of Commons to adjourn on Derby Day, and it was a distinct political advantage to Palmerston that he was popularly acclaimed as a successful race-horse owner. Moreover, the use of the electric telegraph for disseminating " sporting intelligence," and a growing fondness for gambling among the inhabitants of the towns, began to make racing results a matter of increasing concern to people who seldom or perhaps never visited a race-course.

Cricket already enjoyed a position of esteem and distinction in English life, but it was not yet either the skilful or the standardised affair which it was to become later in the century. An item displayed at the Great Exhibition was, for instance, in the words of the catalogue, " a newly invented cricket bat, with flexible handle "—a convenience which posterity has not found necessary. The report in *The Times* of the match between the M.C.C. and Cambridge University in 1851 contained the comment : " And so the University won by 20 runs. Supposing there had been better ' longstopping ' on the part of the M.C.C. this match would have borne a far more satisfactory appearance." The M.C.C. may have had poor longstops, but their bowling seems to have been less lacking in direction than the University's. There were no wides in the Cambridge score, whereas there were 11 in the two innings of the M.C.C., which totalled 207. Cricket had not yet become an international affair, and the principal matches of the cricketing year were the University match, England v. Kent and the Gentlemen v. the Players.

Lords. Cricket was not yet the skilful or standardised affair which it was to become later in the century

Henley Regatta was already a recognised social function, and rowing was a sport which had recently grown in popularity. As Thackeray observed in *The History of Pendennis*, " boat-racing had not risen in Pen's time to the fureur which, as we are given to understand, it has since attained in the university ; and riding and tandem-driving were the fashions of the ingenuous youth." The University Boat Race was an established institution, but it was not yet held every year.

The modern form of boxing, as regulated by the Queensberry rules, was not yet a recognised sport, and prize-fighting in the old style, in which what would now be called fouls were freely exchanged, still survived. Boxing-gloves were used in practice, but prize-fights were still fought with bare fists, the bruisers, as they were called, toughening their hands by soaking them in an astringent solution. Fights ended when a bruiser could not come into the ring at the beginning of a new round. Prize-fighters no longer had the social prestige which they had enjoyed earlier in the century, and the public were becoming more and more repelled by the brutality of their sport. However, boxing of a kind was a popular recreation, especially among the lower orders, and in some taverns landlords hired out gloves for 1d. or 2d. a time.

Swimming had a rather restricted appeal. The habit of visiting the seaside was gaining in popularity : the railway companies were already finding it profitable to run special trains with cheap return fares to holiday resorts, and a Baptist missionary named Thomas Cook had begun to organise excursions for the Midland Railway Company. The needs of swimmers were, however, so little provided for that it was not found necessary to introduce even elementary precautions at the seaside. In August, 1851, two people were drowned at Ramsgate, and regret was expressed in the newspapers that no lifeboats were available such as were provided at Boulogne.

Of the other outdoor games which have since become accepted institutions, golf was still virtually a Scottish monopoly ; lawn tennis had not been invented ; and football, though of ancient origin, was still a somewhat irregular pastime, no generally acceptable rules for either Association or Rugby football having yet been codified.

In short, many varieties of sport were indulged in a hundred years ago by people who happened to be interested in them, and there were then, as there have long been in England, influential circles in which a man was judged primarily by his ability to ride to hounds. Sport as a spectacle for the masses, however, consisted of little more than a few annual outings, such as that of Derby Day.

Yet spectacle was something which the masses wanted, as they showed clearly enough whenever it was offered to them. Circuses, which in their modern form in England date from the opening of Astley's in 1780, were so popular that many theatres had to provide what were virtually circus acts in order to flourish. Crowds flocked to Greenwich Fair every Easter Monday ; Madame Tussaud's was already a popular attraction ; and in August, 1851, 145,000 people visited the London Zoo.

Another well patronised form of spectacle was the exhibition of wonders, which was something of a cross between an art gallery and a fun fair, and which specialised in offering the appeal of the exotic. A representative specimen of this kind of attraction was the Grand Exhibition of Art adjoining the Adelaide Gallery. In 1851 it was advertised in the following terms : " Wonderful Performing Elephant and Automaton Bell-ringer, the size of life—gorgeous Pearl Eaters—superb Temple of Fountains—Automaton Singing Bird, in a cage of pure gold—Serpents and Palm Trees—Lady Organist—Jewelled Theatre—beautiful Cosmoramic Views—5,000 feet of Needlework Pictures. Hatching Chickens. Pianoforte by Miss Butler every evening. Admission 1s., children half-price."

The " Grand Exhibition of Art " would have been regarded in later *fin-de-siècle* circles as a preposterous title for a show of this kind, yet it had certain attributes which large sections of the public expected to find wherever the word " art " was mentioned. To posterity the English graphic arts of the middle of the last century mean primarily the later works of Turner, the water-colours of Samuel Palmer and Edward Lear, or else that remarkable movement whose outstanding products were the works of Rossetti and Ford Madox Brown, of Millais and Holman Hunt. If to-day we visit an exhibition of mid-nineteenth-century painting, we expect, before all else, to see the haunting features of the consumptive Elizabeth Siddall looking down on us ; around her will be displayed that peculiar mastery, which the pre-Raphaelites revealed, in treating subjects which seem to date from the age of Sir Walter Scott with an

The University Boat-race was already an established institution

The Aerial Man

(speaking the Observatory, Greenwich Park.)

Rock & Cᵒ London

Aerial man

Cremorne Gardens still enjoyed considerable popularity

approach to the details of Nature suggestive of the age of Charles Darwin.

The art of the pre-Raphaelites was, however, that of a coterie of young men, who formed themselves into what they called a " brotherhood " in the home of the parents of one of them. Naturally enough, therefore, they were rebels against the popular art of their day, and among the qualities they rebelled against were those which a public, looking before all else for the spectacular, expected artists to provide. The subjects of paintings shown at the Great Exhibition give some indication of what the taste of the time called for : Alexander the Great crossing the Granicus, Little Nell and her grandfather, the peaceful arts triumphing over war, Titania and Oberon. Literary and narrative painting with a moral, historical and, above all, an exotic flavour—this was what popular art a hundred years ago contributed towards spectacular entertainment. They were qualities which no one man, not even the accepted master of the day, Landseer, could combine in such of his work as was to be of lasting value. Perhaps qualities were demanded in art which would not have been demanded had the spectacular been more readily available in other forms.

To some extent the gaps in the provision of public entertainment a hundred years ago were filled by entertainment of a private and social nature. Some of the great houses, for instance, organised theatrical performances. At the Duke of Devonshire's London house in 1851 a distinguished cast included, in addition to Wilkie Collins and Douglas Jerrold, Charles Dickens, who had a pronounced hankering after a stage career, and whom the Duke of Argyll described as a great natural actor. In middle-class homes reading aloud was a popular pastime, and in this activity, too, Dickens had many opportunities for displaying his histrionic talents. Some form of musical accomplishment was expected of young ladies of fashion, and amateurs of one sex or the other showed an interest in a wide range of instruments, some of which to-day have a rather limited appeal. A contemporary advertisement, for instance, in which an offer was made to teach the *cornet à pistons*, described the instrument as " delightful and fashionable."

A much higher degree of skill on the dance floor was also demanded of the middle and upper classes than is expected to-day. Teachers of dancing could rely with some assurance on a steady demand to learn the

The gardens offered attractive spectacles such as ascents in balloons

waltz—or " valse " as it was called—the schottische and the polka. Of
card-games, whist was considered the most suitable in polite circles, but
Mayhew stated that costermongers in general declared it to be dull. The
most popular indoor games among the working classes were shove-
halfpenny, skittles and cribbage in the pubs, and draughts and dominoes
in the coffee-houses.

One form of social entertainment which still survived a hundred years
ago but which virtually disappeared afterwards—although a revival is
now being staged in Battersea Park—was that of the public gardens. Of
these, Cremorne and Vauxhall Gardens still enjoyed considerable
popularity, and they offered attractive spectacles such as fireworks and
ascents in balloons. As centres of fashion for promenading and listening
to music, however, they were already on the decline, and their end was
near. Vauxhall Gardens were closed in 1859, and Cremorne Gardens
in 1877.

On the whole, the verdict which must be passed on entertainment in
Britain a hundred years ago is that the supply was inadequate to meet
the demand. The nation had already become largely urban in character,
and in an urban society the masses look for provision of entertainment
by outside agencies to a far greater extent than they do in the countryside.

In so far as artistic standards are applicable, the level that was reached
in entertainment was also generally low. It is true that great individual
artists were practising. Turner, who died in 1851, painted some of his
greatest pictures in the last ten years of his life ; a master in his own
genre such as George Cruikshank was producing inimitable drawings ;
Mendelssohn chose England as his temporary home and English orchestras
and choirs to launch a number of his works ; and in 1851 Macready and
Samuel Phelps could be seen on the stage, and Jenny Lind was a recent
memory.

Nevertheless, there was only one art form in which great work was
both consistently produced and widely accepted. That form was literature.
To understand why there was such an outpouring of great literature at
a time when the general level of the other arts was so low, it will be
necessary to consider not so much the supply and demand of entertainment, but rather the intellectual temper of the age.

CHAPTER SIX

PROBLEMS OF THE DAY

IT IS always difficult to decide what were the accepted habits of thought of any particular age of the past, and it is especially difficult in the case of an age in which there was such strenuous intellectual activity as there was in mid-Victorian England. For one thing, there is a danger of confusing a general lip-service paid to certain traditional modes of thought with the intellectual orthodoxy of the day. Thus a hundred years ago in England there was a widespread readiness to subscribe to the Anglican form of Christian worship, and the standards set in the more venerable places of learning were designed to encourage that attitude. The subjects chosen for examination at Cambridge in 1851 were the Gospel of St. Matthew ; Paley's *Evidences*; Old Testament history ; the *Iliad*, book 23 ; the first book of Livy ; the *Elements* of Euclid, books 1 and 2 ; and arithmetic.

However, to deduce from this that English thought a hundred years ago was predominantly Christian and, therefore, spiritual in its tendencies would not only be wrong ; it would be very nearly the opposite of the truth. If there was such a thing as orthodox philosophy in England at that time, it took the form firstly of a belief in something called " progress "—a more or less inevitable movement which could be left to the operation of " natural laws "—and secondly of a materialistic, or even a mechanistic, interpretation of the universe. That, at any rate, was what most of its critics, both contemporary and subsequent, believed to be the orthodox philosophy of the age. It was just that philosophy which G. K. Chesterton described when he wrote : " The soul of Bentham (if he had one) went marching on, like John Brown ; and in the central Victorian movement it was certainly he who won. John Stuart Mill was the final flower of that growth. He was himself fresh and delicate and pure ; but that is the business of a flower."

This comment of Chesterton's on John Stuart Mill contained a deeper truth than the mere expression of a personal dislike of the philosophy of Jeremy Bentham and of what Bentham himself called his doctrine of the " utilitarian." It indicated what any analysis of Mill's work must reveal, the direction in which the so-called " advanced " political thinking of the day was moving.

If one word is to be chosen to describe that direction, perhaps the best word which can be found is " socialism." By the middle of the century socialism was a fairly well established doctrine in intellectual circles. Its popular association with atheism still gave it a power to shock. When Charlotte Brontë read the *Letters on the Laws of Man's Social Nature and Development*, which Harriet Martineau and Henry Atkinson published in 1851, the essential governess rose up in her, and she described it as " the first exposition of avowed atheism and materialism I have ever read." Nevertheless, socialism already had a relatively respectable Christian wing. This included a professor of English literature and history at King's College, London, in F. D. Maurice, although it is true that in 1851 his Principal called on him to clear himself of charges of religious heterodoxy which the *Quarterly Review* had brought against him.

The belief in progress being what it was, political theorists a hundred years ago were beginning to accept the view that socialism was simply the extension and culmination of liberalism. Indeed, even to-day, although empirical tests may be thought to have revealed the fundamental cleavage between the two philosophies, this curiously Victorian view still survives. Its survival is shown by the use in political circles of the word " progressive " by people who in other respects, somewhat illogically, lay no claim to the gift of clairvoyance.

A hundred years ago liberals and socialists both subscribed to the doctrine of progress. Marx, who by the middle of the century had not yet become a serious intellectual force in England, was so strongly influenced by his belief in progress that he regarded the triumph of the proletariat as something which must inevitably emerge from the capitalist system. Mill also expressed considerable confidence in the future victory of what he regarded as a superior social organisation. The true essence of the Fabian philosophy is indeed to be found in Mill's *Autobiography*, in which, when describing his political development about the middle of the century, he wrote: " The social problem of the future we considered to be, how to unite the greatest individual liberty of action, with a common ownership of the raw material of the globe." Mill's own intellectual development from the philosophy of *laissez-faire*, which had so strongly influenced his father, to that of a rather Fabian socialism was indeed a perfectly logical and orderly one, and his admirers saw no reason why a similar progress should not be general.

To both liberals and socialists, the main work which seemed necessary

VERY LIKE A WHALE !
The French Socialist Leading the British Lion by the Nose.
DEDICATED TO OUR YANKEE WELL-WISHERS.

Socialism was a fairly well established doctrine

a hundred years ago in order that mankind might come into its proper heritage, lay in the field of education. Their relative confidence or lack of confidence in the speed with which education could be efficacious served to distinguish one kind of political partisan from another. Marx overcame the educational obstacle with a clear leap and assumed that the proletariat would exercise power benevolently. Mill, on the other hand, had his doubts. Again referring to the middle of the century in his *Autobiography*, he wrote : " In short I was a democrat, but not the least of a Socialist. We were now much less democrats than I had been, because so long as education continues to be so wretchedly imperfect, we dreaded the ignorance and especially the selfishness and brutality of the mass."

The imperfection of contemporary education did indeed temper the optimism of some of the progressives. Yet even in this field they saw hopeful signs about them, for there were plenty of indications that literacy at least was on the increase. Mudie's library was a growing concern in the forties ; W. H. Smith and Son opened their first railway bookstall at Euston in 1848 ; the first Public Libraries Act was passed in 1850 ; and a working man's college, which had been founded by F. D. Maurice, was flourishing. It was at this college that the Duke of Argyll heard a working man ask the question : " Why should another man be entitled to make a profit out of my labour ? " Something of the intellectual climate of the age is revealed in the fact that the Duke, a distinguished politician, had the honesty to admit that he could not find a convincing answer to the question.

In short, though it would be a fallacy to suppose that in the middle of the last century socialism was an orthodox philosophy among intellectuals to anything like the extent that it was, for instance, in the nineteen-thirties—deep-rooted beliefs were far too strong to allow that to be the case—yet a form of liberalism, one of whose outcomes was already seen to be socialism, was a creed which was gaining wider and wider acceptance. Outside the political sphere this creed was associated with a particular kind of materialism, which, by various feats of manipulation, was harnessed to the precepts of Christianity. In these tenets of belief, if anywhere, was to be found the intellectual orthodoxy of the age.

However, even if this general definition of orthodoxy is accepted, many of the most interesting and original thinkers a hundred years ago were, it must be admitted, people who rebelled against it. To some extent a tendency of this kind has been apparent in nearly all periods of recent history ; yet the 'very strength of the revolt against the orthodox was itself a characteristic of English thought in the middle of the last century. It was a revolt which was expressed in religion and literature, in philosophy and the natural sciences, at a time when in the majority of European countries there were political revolts of a more physical nature against other forms of orthodoxy.

Of the intellectual rebels of the day, those whose utterances gave rise to the most passionate controversies in thoughtful circles were naturally the religious ones. Religious heterodoxy could still inspire that sensation of horror which in a later age and in different circumstances has accrued to political deviation. The age being a relatively tolerant one, religious deviators did not suffer very painful consequences, but they were still regarded with feelings of fascination and even of awe.

A decade before the Great Exhibition the interest aroused by the Oxford Movement had been intense. Newman had been able to pack St. Mary's with congregations consisting largely of undergraduates who came to hear his sermons, and he could even hold well-attended communion services at 7 a.m. Ninety-five editions of Keble's *Christian Year* were, moreover, sold during the author's lifetime.

By 1851 the Oxford Movement had virtually come to an end, for its leader had been lost six years earlier, when Newman was received into the Church of Rome. However, though the movement itself had become disorganised, the spirit of rebellion against prevailing trends of thought, which to some extent it represented, was very much alive. It had even gained additional strength from new loyalties and new associations. Newman's conversion to Rome was indeed the logical outcome of all his earlier thoughts and actions, as many of his contemporary critics had long appreciated. Thomas Arnold of Rugby had once stated : " My feelings towards a Roman Catholic are quite different from my feelings towards a Newmanite, because I think the one a fair enemy, the other a treacherous one. The one is a Frenchman in his own uniform . . . the other is a Frenchman disguised in a red coat." It may not have been a very graceful comment on the outstanding religious figure of the age, but at least it showed an accurate intuition.

The theological considerations which justified Newman in his act of conversion arose from his studies of early Christian heresies, but there were sociological considerations which influenced him equally strongly. He had long been dissatisfied with the role which the Established Church was playing in the spiritual life of the nation, and he had noticed a tendency on the part of the religious-minded to join other sects " because the Church does not provide innocent outlets for the sober relief of feeling and excitement." Intellectually, too, he was opposed to the growing habit of approaching religious or indeed social problems with a mental attitude more suited to the study of mathematics. This, he felt, gave rise to a danger of confusing the absolute truths of the exact sciences, which could be discovered by " rigid demonstration," and the relative social truths, which could be reached only by the evidence of " accumulated probabilities."

Cardinal Newman

Moreover, the social scene which he looked out upon, particularly after he left Oxford, disposed him to believe not in a steady upward progression of mankind but in something very different. " The human race," he wrote

in his *Apologia*, " is implicated in some terrible aboriginal calamity. It is
out of joint with the purposes of its Creator. This is a fact, a fact as true
as the fact of its existence; and thus the doctrine of what is theologically
called original sin becomes to me almost as certain as that the world
exists, and as the existence of God." Dean Stanley once expressed the
opinion that things would have been very different if only Newman had
known German—by which he meant the work of the German theologians.
It might perhaps have been even truer if he had said that things would
have been very different if only Newman had not known Birmingham.

Newman in 1851 was lecturing in the Birmingham Corn Exchange on the
rather delicate problem of " the present position of Catholics in England."
His popularity was at one of its lowest ebbs, and he did not regain a high
position in popular esteem until the next decade, after the publication of
his *Apologia*. Nevertheless, the intellectual movement towards Catholicism,
of which in some ways he was the leader, was gaining in strength. This
does not mean that popular, emotional antipapism was on the decline.
Indeed, when the Ecclesiastical Titles Bill was being debated in Parliament
in 1851, this feeling was given a new spur, and numerous " petitions
against Papal aggression " were sent to the House of Lords; yet at the
very time that these petitions were pouring in, Manning was following
Newman's example of conversion to Rome, and the great Catholic
literary movement, which has been such a remarkable feature of English
thought during the last hundred years, and which was one of the most
powerful expressions of the revolt against materialism, had already begun.

There were a number of other important movements within religious
bodies in the forties of a more or less breakaway character. There
was the secession from the Scottish Church led by Chalmers; the dis-
ruptive movement among the Methodists led by Everett, Griffith and
Dunn; and the formation of the group of Christian Socialists. The
chief cause of all these movements was, however, a desire for an extension of democracy in Church or State Government. They therefore
led in the same direction as many of the prevailing trends of political
thought and not, as Newman was moving, in a diametrically opposite
direction. The Low Church secessionists and the Christian Socialists
did not, like Newman, believe that the false promises of Antichrist
were equality, trade, wealth and the remission of taxes; and they did

A PRETTY KETTLE OF FISH.

Puseyite Parson. "What! Want to leave your Situation! Why, I thought you were Perfectly Satisfied?"

Cook. "Well, Sir, the fact is, I ain't equal to them Fast Days; for what with a Hegg here, and a Hegg there, and little bits o' Fish for Breakfastes, and little bits o' Fish for Dinners, and the Sweet Omelicks, and the Fried and the Stewed Hoysters, and the Bashawed Lobsterses, and one think and the hother, there's so much Cooking, that I ain't even time to make up a Cap!"

Puseyite parson and his cook

not share Newman's profound doubts about the beneficence of the existing political system and of the changes which were being effected in it.

Newman was in many respects a romantic, and in his political views he had much in common with some of the leading romantic writers of his age. The great romantic movement in English literature, which had reached its height in the early part of the nineteenth century, had been individual and lyrical rather than social and didactic in its expression. Shelley, it is true, had written extensively about politics, but his political opinions, in spite of his own remarkable intellectual powers, could hardly be regarded as adult. Blake, through an intuitive process, had come to make pronouncements of great political wisdom, but so in its own day had the Delphic oracle, and neither was easily appreciated by contemporaries. Of the earlier masters of the romantic lyric, Wordsworth alone survived until 1850, but in his declining years, though he might write a sonnet in protest against the building of the Kendal-Windermere railway, he did not concern himself with any comprehensive criticism of the contemporary social scene.

What may be called the second or neo-romantic movement in English literature and the other arts, a movement which was in progress in the middle of the century, was by contrast one in which there was a strong social consciousness. Its most popular medium was the novel, an essentially social art-form. Among the poets, too, Browning reached his highest flights not in the treatment of private emotions but in the creation of a vast gallery of characters, most of them portrayed in moments of acute social conflict. Neither Browning nor the majority of the greater novelists, however, deep though their concern with social problems was, could be described as primarily interested in politics. Carlyle, on the other hand, was a politician in everything except practice, and it is in his works rather than anywhere else that a statement of the romantic political revolt is to be found.

By 1851 Carlyle had become the author of *Past and Present* and the *Latter-Day Pamphlets*. He had ceased to be the young enthusiast of Craigenputtock and was in the process of becoming the sage of Chelsea, a translation which was of questionable benefit to his literary work. However, though the *Latter-Day Pamphlets* already suggested much of

Carlyle's latter-day petulance, they also contained some of his most devastating criticism of the contemporary social scene.

For Carlyle, as for Newman, the contemporary social scene justified neither satisfaction with the present nor optimism about the immediate future. Indeed, to justify optimism even about a distant future, Carlyle had to evolve his doctrine that " Might and Right do differ frightfully from hour to hour ; but give them centuries to try it in, they are found to be identical." For the present, the chief physical creation of the new civilisation seemed to him " the immeasurable Steam-engine " ; its most vaunted social product was the " Aristocracy of the Money-bag . . . a baser sort of Aristocracy . . . an infinitely baser ; the basest yet known " ; and its spiritual atmosphere was a " whole baleful cunningly-compacted Universe of Cant." Formula had become a substitute for religion, and appeals to self-interest or to conflicting interests the whole of politics. Such measures as the Repeal of the Corn Laws could, he felt, provide only a temporary alleviation of discontent, and even the apparently philanthropic acitivities of prison reform and crusades against slavery seemed to him merely sops to dishonestly controlled consciences. Moreover, the whole doctrine of the liberal economists of reducing interference by the State to a minimum was, he believed, based on false premises ; for him the State had a duty to provide something more than " Anarchy *plus* a constable."

As a critic of the contemporary social scene, Carlyle was in many ways supreme. That brilliant phrase, " Liberty to die by Starvation," which has remained the best weapon in the intellectual armoury of totalitarians for a century, originates from him, and there was scarcely one defect in the civilisation of his day on which he did not fasten with a clear vision and an unequalled power of expression. It is when we consider the alternatives he had to offer to that civilisation that we find an emptiness, an emptiness which may, at bottom, have been as disturbing to him as his dyspepsia or the distress which he genuinely felt at existing conditions.

Carlyle's early mental struggles in Edinburgh, which had led him to discard the Calvinistic belief in the literal truth of the Bible on which he had been brought up, left their mark on him for the rest of his life. He was continually seeking a faith. For many years he believed he had found that faith in the works of Goethe, in which he steeped himself, yet there was in the end a surprising divergence between his own attitude to life and that of his master. In so far as he adopted a philosophy from the Germans, it was rather that curiously German Protestant doctrine of grace in preference to works, and of the power of the spirit within the individual which sets him above man-made laws.

This doctrine, though it was as readily voiced by Adolf Hitler as by Luther, by Schiller's first gangster-hero as by the best of the German romantics, is at least intellectually defensible. It is difficult to say the same about the practical steps which Carlyle recommended for the implementation of his philosophy. Most of these steps were indeed to be taken readily enough later in the country which he so deeply admired, Germany. Aggressive racialism in dealing with what he called " the nigger problem," belief in militarism and especially the drill-sergeant— even to the point of advocating compulsory drill as a suitable exercise for English Bank Holiday crowds—admiration of Prussia and all the trappings of the *Führerprinzip*—every one of these is to be found in Carlyle's positive expressions of belief. There is, too, something rather appalling in his condemnation of his fellow-countrymen's " despair of finding any Heroes to govern you and contented putting-up with the want of them." The contempt implied in the use of the word " contented " is only too revealing.

Although his admiration of all things German, an admiration which he even carried to the point of writing most English nouns with a capital initial letter, led Carlyle to embrace many articles of a rather unattractive creed, his very respect for foreign modes of thought was at least salutory in mid-nineteenth-century England. A gentler but no less searching critic of the mid-Victorian world, Matthew Arnold, some years later did rather more to break down the strong national isolation of English thought, but in places he followed where Carlyle had led. However, in spite of this incidental benefit which he conferred, Carlyle's main contribution to the political thought of his day must be considered the voicing, with devastating clarity, of doubts about the rightness of the course which contemporary economists, politicians and philosophers were advocating, doubts which were felt by a number of his fellow-men and particularly his fellow-artists.

One way in which certain of the writers and other artists of Carlyle's day expressed their doubts about the beneficence of the existing social scene was by showing an increasing interest in the distant past. It is a widespread romantic habit to look towards the distant past, for one of the qualities of romanticism is to prefer what-is-not to what-is. A hundred years ago there was, it is true, a remarkable output of great novels concerned with the immediate present, but the devotees of the distant past were also both numerous and influential. Evidence of this cult is to be found, for example, in the works of Ruskin, in the paintings of the pre-Raphaelites, and in the Celtic literary revival, which was precipitated by Lady Charlotte Guest's translation of the ancient Welsh prose tales known as the *Mabinogion*.

That these expressions of romanticism were also in part expressions of a political revolt is shown by their social rather than individual character. Ruskin did not look to the past simply as at something colourful and picturesque ; he suggested that medievalism should be closely examined in order that ways might be found of introducing the merits of medievalism into contemporary society. In this respect he served as a spokesman of the feelings of a number of the pre-Raphaelites, even of Ford Madox Brown, who was sufficiently in harmony with the progressives to confess to what he called " twinges of socialism." The Celtic revivalists, too, believed that something could be found in the Welsh past which was lacking in the Welsh or English present.

The participants in these literary and artistic movements were only incidentally politicians, and they did not enunciate a political philosophy as articulately as Carlyle did. Yet in their attitude to society they differed profoundly from the so-called " advanced " political thinkers, whose main criticism of contemporary society was that it was not moving far enough and fast enough in the direction in which it was already being propelled.

While the progressives were looking forward to a steady upward advance by mankind, and Newman and Carlyle, Ruskin and Matthew Arnold were voicing doubts of different kinds, a new revolution was occurring in English thought which had immensely far-reaching consequences. This revolution took place in the field of the natural sciences.

The civilisation which had arisen from the growth of industry during the preceding hundred years had become more and more the civilisation of the machine, of Carlyle's " immeasurable Steam-engine." In consequence there had been a growing tendency to assume that the laws of machines were applicable to the whole of the universe. Carlyle, as in so many other cases, had seized upon this particular intellectual weakness and had complained of " the mechanical style " of the treatment of the major mysteries of life. In the same way Matthew Arnold was to com-

Experimental exhibition of electric light in Trafalgar Square

plain " how entirely does the narrow and mechanical conception of our secular business proceed from a narrow and mechanical conception of our religious business." It was perhaps unfortunate that as an alternative to the " mechanical " Carlyle offered the " dynamic," a word which by emotional and even political associations has acquired a misleading significance. Scientists, however, used another and more appropriate word to describe a new attitude towards the mysteries of Nature. This was the word " organic."

In 1844 a book had appeared entitled *Vestiges of the Natural History of Creation.* Its effect was sensational, for in a scientific and convincing manner it undermined belief in the literal truth of the story of Genesis. There was prolonged and keen speculation on the identity of the author, and eventually he was discovered as Robert Chambers. Fifteen years later, when Darwin brought out his *Origin of Species,* much less sensation was caused, for the intellectual world, at least, had already been prepared to some extent for the doctrine of evolution.

One of the characteristics of the mechanical civilisation had been a tendency to regard science as a means whereby man could triumph over Nature, rather than as a knowledge which could help him to understand and adapt himself to natural forces. In consequence the period during which this attitude of mind had prevailed had been one of spoliation and of disregard of the penalties which follow from a denial of the essential nature of the earth and of man's own being. The hewing of coal wherever it was most conveniently placed, deforestation, and the plunder of virgin soil were all found to be necessary operations, and little thought was given to their long-term effect on the earth's resources. Similarly, the less fortunate victims of the industrial system had been forced into unnatural conditions of darkness and squalor. At the same time even the well-to-do had acquired the habit of denying themselves sunlight, and they gradually developed an abnormal shame of many of their bodily functions.

The doctrine of evolution was only one expression of the revolt against this mechanistic view of life, a revolt which took the form of considering the organic nature of animal—including human animal—vegetable, and mineral development, and of drawing the logical conclusions. The growing interest shown in geology in the forties was a symptom of

McCormick's mechanical reaper

the same tendency ; so were early studies on the subject of soil erosion and the budding science of psychology.

This new attitude towards Nature also began to be revealed in a number of the inventions of the age. Mr. Lewis Mumford has convincingly shown how much was owed in the second half of the nineteenth century, even in mechanical inventions, to a realistic appreciation of natural design. Thus it would hardly have been possible to invent the telephone without a study of the structure of the human ear, nor to develop the modern aeroplane from the various flying-machines produced in the middle of the century without a study of the manner in which birds fly.

Around the middle of the century a number of the most important inventions made were still largely mechanical in kind—that is to say, they did not require an organic, as opposed to a mechanistic, conception of Nature for their consummation to be possible. Such were the typewriter, the modern high-speed sewing-machine and the modern safety-match, all of which date at least in experimental form from the forties, although not all originated in England. Such, too, was McCormick's mechanical reaper, which was shown at the Great Exhibition.

On the other hand, inventions of immense future significance were being made in other fields, which were the direct outcome either of a close study of the human organism, or else of a realisation of the possibilities of harnessing new forms of energy from natural resources. Such were the inventions in the fields of anæsthetics and electricity.

It was a characteristic of these inventions that, unlike many of the earlier mechanical ones, they were almost exclusively beneficial to mankind, and did not have socially damaging by-products. Simpson's use of chloroform as an anæsthetic, for instance, led to a revolution in surgery and served—perhaps more than any other discovery in human history—to reduce the physical sufferings of mankind. The numerous discoveries of Faraday in the field of electricity and the invention of the electric arc-light, which was patented in 1846, also brought incalculable benefits. Like advances which were being made in another field, in the development of the modern photograph from the old daguerreotype, they were, in their social significance, symptoms of a new appreciation of light, an element which the mining age had done so much to banish from working and living conditions.

The revolt against the mechanistic, and the readiness to conform to the organic conception of Nature was, of course, a movement which it is impossible to date other than approximately ; but it can at least be said that about the middle of the century the movement was beginning to make noticeable headway. Like the other intellectual revolts of the time which have been analysed, its consequences are to-day still apparent. Whether Newman was right in insisting on the need for a Catholic revival ; whether the evolutionists were right in calling for a new understanding of the forces of Nature ; whether Carlyle was right in decrying contemporary liberalism, or Mill right in believing it must develop into socialism ; these must be matters of opinion. All that can be said with certainty is that it is to such movements as those which have been analysed, and the further movements to which they in turn gave rise, that we owe many of the differences between the intellectual atmosphere of our own day and that which prevailed a hundred years ago.

Just how great those differences are, is a question which seems more difficult to answer the more closely one considers it. Sometimes, when for instance one compares the political doctrines of Mill or Carlyle with modern party manifestos, the differences seem slight. At other times, as when one considers the flurry that was caused by Chambers's *Vestiges*, the gulf appears enormous.

In the end, perhaps the simplest way of assessing the extent of these differences will be found to be the casting of a glance at some work which can legitimately be regarded as an outstanding product of the intellectual orthodoxy of the middle of the last century. From this we may be able to decide how many of the conflicts described are those of our own day and how many are obviously period pieces. As suitable a work as any for this purpose would be—appropriately enough in view of the success with which the author was to fill the part of mid-Victorian Poet Laureate—Tennyson's *In Memoriam*.

It is immediately apparent, for instance, that *In Memoriam* is strongly influenced by contemporary evolutionary theories. The evolutionary picture which Tennyson accepts is that of a steady upward progression of life, and not the grimmer picture of a relentless struggle for existence which filled the minds of many later Victorians. Man is seen as Nature's " last work," and he must " move upwards, working out the beast, and let the ape and tiger die." A strong sense of social duty is equally apparent throughout the work. Although it is an expression of deep personal sorrow, there is no suggestion of *Weltschmerz* or of the unhappy individual romantic oppressed by society :

> " *Is this an hour*
> *For private sorrow's barren song,*
> *When more and more the people throng*
> *The chairs and thrones of civil power ?*
>
> *A time to sicken and to swoon,*
> *When Science reaches forth her arms*
> *To feel from world to world, and charms*
> *Her secret from the latest moon ? "*

Time and again, however, there recurs in the poem a feeling of religious doubt, " the slender shade of doubt " in the mind of one whose " faith is dry." As far as the weaker female vessel, the poet's sister, is concerned, duty clearly indicates that she should not be troubled with doubts but left to enjoy " when she prays, her early Heaven." For Tennyson and Hallam, however, a more exacting—perhaps the appropriate word is a

The original Singer sewing-machine

more "manly"—struggle is necessary. In the end the conventional religious faith, as expressed in a belief in the Resurrection, wins with a triumphant cry : "And I shall know him when we meet." However, we feel all along that it has been a close contest, and the evident attractions of the idealised picture of the country rectory have clearly made a major contribution to the triumph.

On analysis, it will be seen that many of Tennyson's conflicts are

those of our own day, and to that extent the intellectual atmospheres of
the two ages appear surprisingly similar. Where the great gulf is to be
found is in the difference between the readiness shown a hundred years
ago and the readiness shown to-day to find an acceptable solution to
these conflicts. This is what makes the conclusion inescapable that the
mid-Victorian age, for all its philosophic and religious doubts, for all its
searching criticism of contemporary society, was fundamentally an
optimistic one.

" Let knowledge grow from more to more, but more of reverence in
us dwell "—that is the battle-cry of the age of the Great Exhibition. We
to-day have our doubts about the growth of knowledge, perhaps even
of the value of knowledge ; we certainly have little evidence of an increase
in reverence, and we may not think reverence particularly desirable.
A hundred years ago these doubts were not unknown, but one of the

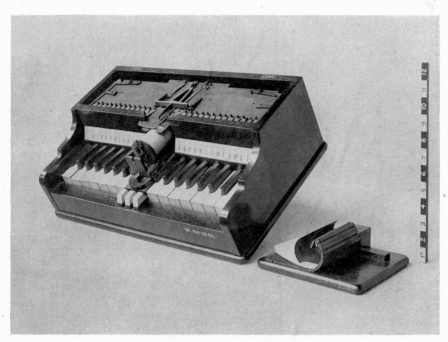

One of the earliest typewriters

strengths of the mid-Victorians was a much greater facility for exorcising them. Knowledge and reverence certainly did not seem incompatible ; nobody found Tennyson ludicrous or offensive ; and, perhaps most important of all, few people thought his ideals unlikely to be realised. Progress, in short, however one cared to define it, seemed to be part of the natural order of things.

CHAPTER SEVEN

THE WORLD ABROAD

WHEN allotting floor space for the Great Exhibition, the Commissioners decided that the following European and partly European countries should be represented in addition to Great Britain : Austria, Belgium, Denmark, France, Germany, Greece, Holland, Italy, Norway and Sweden jointly, Portugal, Russia, Spain, Switzerland and Turkey. Within the space allotted to Germany there was a sub-division into the states of the Steuerverein, the two Mecklenburgs, the Hanse towns and the Zollverein. Italy was similarly sub-divided into Naples, Rome, Sardinia and Tuscany. The independent countries or territories invited from the American continent were Bolivia, Brazil, Buenos Aires, Central America, Chile, Ecuador, Mexico, Montevideo, New Granada, Peru, the United States and Venezuela. Other countries from which exhibits were expected were Arabia, China, Egypt, Morocco, Persia, Tunis and West Africa. Contributions were also invited from a large number of British colonies.

By their selection of possible participants, the Commissioners thus gave expression to a fact which most European politicians of the time were still somewhat reluctant to recognise. A hundred years ago it was the common practice to regard foreign politics as almost exclusively an affair of maintaining the balance of power in Europe. This attitude of mind had prevailed at the Congress of Vienna ; it survived in some quarters down to the year 1938, when its death-pangs were expressed in the choice of countries to be represented at the Munich meeting ; and only in the last few years, when two non-European or predominantly non-European states have come to be recognised as the major world powers, can it be said to have disappeared.

Nevertheless, one of the inescapable facts of nineteenth-century history was the rapid development of countries outside Europe. By the middle of the century the process of creating an inter-continental dependence, which was later to be accelerated by the radio and the aeroplane, had already been begun by the railway and the steamship. Large-scale emigration had also been going on long enough for the inhabitants of various territories in America and Australasia to have established new ways of life of their own. Politicians concerned with the major problems of diplomacy could still regard the non-European countries as colonial or semi-colonial territories, or else to consider them sufficiently far removed from the centre of political gravity for their affairs to be of secondary importance. To those who were engaged in trade, however, the importance of non-European countries was more immediately obvious. This importance was first brought home to large sections of the British public by the riches which they saw displayed at the Great Exhibition. In particular, a new awareness was formed of the extent and wealth of Britain's own possessions overseas.

The forties and fifties were years in which events of the greatest importance in shaping the constitution of the British Empire of the future occurred. In a number of British colonies the logical conclusions of the repeal of the Corn Laws and the free trade movement were accepted with remarkable realism and speed. Once the differential duties which had protected trade between the colonies and the mother country had been removed, the main justification for regarding territories such as Canada and Australia as trading appendages, which could be wholly governed from London, disappeared. A number of the colonial governors and the administrators at home, realising what this meant, shaped their actions accordingly.

AUSTRALIA IN 1851

For Australia an Act passed by the British Parliament in 1850 meant that constitutions for Victoria, South Australia and Van Diemen's Land, as Tasmania was still called, all came into effect in 1851. One consequence of this was that the new social and economic problems, to which the opening-up of the first Australian goldfield in the same year gave rise, could be approached with a settled administration. The country was thus spared the disturbances which might well have accompanied agitation for a greater degree of independence. Before the first gold rush, which followed from the 1851 discovery, Australia was still a sparsely populated country. Census figures for 1850-51 showed the number of inhabitants of New South Wales as 187,000, of Victoria as 77,000, of Van Diemen's Land as 69,000, of South Australia as 64,000, and of Queensland as a mere 9,000. Most of the settlements had become reasonably orderly. In November, 1850, Lord Ashley had stated that female emigrants could safely be sent to almost all places in the British colonies except Sydney, " the vilest and most corrupt place on the face of the earth." Transportation of convicts to Van Diemen's Land had not come to an end by 1851, but it was to do so two years later, and one of the strongest arguments advanced in favour of ending it was that very discovery of gold, which was to play such a major part in Australian life in the next decade.

CANADA

In Canada the middle of the century was a period in which considerable progress was made towards the consolidation of a nation, which before then had seemed likely to accept a division into two separate entities. The union of Upper and Lower Canada had been given statutory force by the Act of Union of 1840, and one of the measures which most effectively mitigated inter-territorial and inter-racial ill-will was the Act of Indemnification of 1849. In the year 1851 the Governor-General was Lord Elgin, whose policy was largely the maintenance of the tradition of his distinguished predecessor, Lord Durham. Durham had submitted to the authorities at home a blueprint for representative government in Canada, and the influence of his views was reflected in a significant document sent by Lord John Russell to the Lieutenant-Governor of Nova Scotia, in which he compared the functions of a governor with those of a constitutional monarch.

NEW ZEALAND

The most rapid change from the status of a colonial dependency to that of a relatively independent nation was, however, made in New Zealand. It was only in 1840, shortly after the establishment of the first English settlements, that the agreement known as the Treaty of Waitangi was reached with the Maoris. By this treaty the Maori chiefs recognised the Queen's sovereignty and were confirmed in possession of their own lands. Eleven years later not only were there settlements of the New Zealand Company at Wellington, Taranaki, Nelson, Wanganui, Otago and Canterbury, in addition to the missionary settlement at Auckland; but William Fox in London was representing to Her Majesty's Government the need for a charter of self-government for New Zealand. During the intervening period the financial difficulties confronting the settlers of the New Zealand Company—many of which were attributed to the policy of maintaining the Maori system of land tenure—had been largely overcome by the purchase of virtually uninhabited land in the South Island. The price paid was often no more than a shilling a square mile. The future prosperity of New Zealand had also been provided for by the importation and breeding of sheep to such an extent that by 1851 there were some quarter of a million sheep on the islands.

SOUTH AFRICA

In contrast with the peaceful and enduring solution of differences between white settlers and the indigenous population which occurred in New Zealand, and in contrast, too, with the relatively amicable union effected between the descendants of two different European races in Canada, South Africa a hundred years ago showed increasing signs of disturbance. The battle of Boomplatz had been fought in 1848, and Pretorius and his followers had found themselves obliged to cross the Vaal River. This movement was in effect a continuation of the Boer treks which had begun a dozen years earlier. Anti-British feeling among the Boers was aggravated by the British policy of insisting on the equality of Hottentots and white men at law, and of enforcing the use of English as the sole official language ; and disturbances in native affairs were such that British forces were at open war with the Kaffirs from 1850 to 1853.

Cape Mounted Rifles attacking Kaffirs

INDIA

In India the middle of the century was also a period of more than usual unrest. Two wars against the Sikhs had been fought in the forties, and that they had ended in the triumph of forces under British command had been in considerable measure due to the treachery of some of the Sikhs' leaders. One of the indirect consequences of the Sikh wars was the virtually outright sale of the predominantly Moslem country of Kashmir to the Rajput Gulab Singh, an action whose consequences are manifest to-day. Frontier incidents occurring towards the end of 1851 were paving the way for war in Burma the next year, and extensions of British territory were secured by the annexation of the Punjab in 1849 and by a somewhat high-handed action which led to the annexation of Satara.

The period was, in short, one in which the British, under the able direction of Lord Dalhousie, the youngest man to have been appointed to the post of Governor-General, pursued their objectives in India with remarkable energy. While new provinces were annexed on the one hand, on the other hand strenuous campaigns were conducted to eliminate the three social practices in India which the British found most distressing— the burning of widows, female infanticide, and the burying alive of lepers. It was, too, an age in which individual Englishmen wielded extraordinary powers. Herbert Edwardes, recalling the period, described how Henry Lawrence would send young men out to govern a tract of country half the size of England with no other instructions than the precepts : " Settle the country ; make the people happy ; and take care there are no rows."

In so far as it is possible to define British policy a hundred years ago in the countries which were later to become the self-governing Dominions of the British Empire, it may be said that in those territories in which white settlers provided a large proportion of the population a limited form of self-government was rapidly becoming a reality ; elsewhere the tendency was towards an extension of British rule. In each case the decisive considerations were those of trade. In countries where there was a large indigenous population the flag was following and securing trade —a more natural and orderly sequence of events than the reverse process which was popularised in the slogan of a later age. Elsewhere free trade was opening up a new era in the history of British overseas possessions, an era in which independent nationhoods were being created more peacefully than might have been possible had protection and its natural consequences remained in force.

U.S.A.

Unlike the colonies which had remained under British rule, the United States a hundred years ago had already become a powerful nation with a tradition of three-quarters of a century of independence. However, it would hardly have occurred to European statesmen of the time to consider the interests of the United States seriously in any matter not directly affecting the Western Hemisphere. American politicians, imbued with the doctrine of avoiding European entanglements, themselves subscribed to this attitude.

By the middle of the century the United States had for the greater part already passed out of that age of spacious individualism aptly summed up in the dictum of Nicholas Macon, which Mr. Arthur Schlesinger quotes, that " no man should live where he can hear his neighbour's dog bark." The reforms of the Democratic party under Andrew Jackson had made their contribution towards shaping the political structure of the country, and the American nation was already confronted with the burning moral, economic and political issue of slavery. It was in 1850 that the famous compromise on slavery was reached, whereby the newly acquired state of California was to be free soil, but slavery was to be permitted in New Mexico and Utah.

Neither of the leading American parties had committed itself absolutely on the slavery issue by the middle of the century. Polk, the successful Democratic candidate for the Presidency in 1844, who had been returned on an election programme of reduced tariffs, an independent treasury, the settlement of the Oregon boundary problem, and the acquisition of California, had described the " agitation of the slavery question " as " mischievous and wicked." In the 1848 election neither General Zachary Taylor of the Whigs, who died in office and was succeeded by President Fillmore, nor Lewis Cass of the Democrats satisfied the abolitionists.

The forties had been a period of ups and downs for both the Whigs and the Democrats, and as the slavery issue came more and more into the foreground, a widespread realignment of party loyalties took place. A new party known as Free Soil emerged, and at the same time there was a movement into the Democratic camp of a number of Whigs who did not support the immediate abolition of slavery.

Although party loyalties were somewhat confused, the popular excitement aroused by elections increased from contest to contest. By the middle of the century songs and torchlight processions had already become an essential part of the process of electing a President ; the myth, which Lincoln was later to inherit and enhance, that the natural home of every President must be a log-cabin, had already been invented ; and even the

THE VIRGINIAN SLAVE.

INTENDED AS A COMPANION TO POWER'S "GREEK SLAVE."

The burning moral issue of slavery

technique of the town gang had been perfected by Mike Walsh, who called it "the subterranean democracy."

With or without ballyhoo, it was already clear by the middle of the century that the slavery issue was dominating American home politics, and it was to continue to do so until the outbreak of the Civil War. To many Americans, moreover, the full poignancy of the slavery issue was brought home by the publication in 1851 of Harriet Beecher Stowe's *Uncle Tom's Cabin.*

Throughout the forties large-scale immigration into the United States had been taking place, and the discovery of gold in California helped to increase the stream of immigrants at the end of the decade. At the same time political disturbances in Europe were providing cogent reasons for thousands of Europeans to seek homes and freedom in the United States.

The Europe from which people were emigrating in such large numbers a hundred years ago was a continent in which there was a strong community of spirit as well as a striking uniformity of political experiences.

The physical means of travel between one European country and another were somewhat less efficient than they are to-day, and people availed themselves of those means in smaller numbers. On the other hand, artificial barriers between nations were also fewer, and currents of thought, as opposed to mere slogans, could circulate with a correspondingly greater freedom.

Thus it was with a sincere expression of shock that *The Times* complained of the sudden institution of an " execrable system," whereby passports were required for travel within France by Frenchmen and for entry into France by foreigners. Pointing out that Louis Napoleon had himself lived in England, *The Times* declared : " Does he not know it as a fact that Frenchmen, Italians, Spaniards, Germans, Russians do, and the Hivites and Hittites might, if these nationalities still obtained, wander about England at their pleasure without being subjected to the disgusting annoyance of a cloud of impure agents of the police ? . . . Neither upon political grounds nor as a measure of police, is the maintenance of the passport system maintainable for one instant of time."

In this Europe, in which passports were regarded as a deplorable and temporary novelty, a series of disturbances, of revolutions and counter-revolutions, occurred during the years 1848-1851. Although strongly influenced by national feelings, they yet formed part of a movement which in many respects was a super-national and thus a truly European one.

FRANCE

Although the first of the European rebellions in the year 1848 broke out in Sicily, the country which was generally regarded as giving the lead to the European political movements of the time was that to which numerous Europeans had long looked for political inspiration, namely France. In February, 1848, the French monarchy was overthrown after some rather small-scale street fighting in Paris, and Louis-Philippe abdicated in the face of what he described as " une insurrection morale." In December, 1851, Louis Napoleon effected the *coup d'état* which enabled him to proclaim the next year the restoration of the Empire. The political story of the intervening years was that of the failure in practice of a number of temporary expedients.

Among the principal causes of the collapse of the Government which had supported the French monarchy had been the inability of the parties of the centre to reconcile their differences, and their neglect of the dangers which threatened them from their extreme wings—a tendency which has recurred with remarkable frequency in French politics. A subsidiary cause of the collapse had been the revelation in 1847 of some rather unsavoury scandals connected with salt-mine concessions, and when the crisis had come the next year, the Government had shown a fatal lack of confidence in the allegiance of the National Guard.

After the revolution of 1848 the Government of the poet Lamartine, which had been hopefully projected into power, suffered in its efficiency from its triumphant gesture in introducing universal male suffrage and a secret ballot—a dangerous step for revolutionaries to take at any time, and one which the more realistic revolutionaries of later ages have been careful to avoid. The ballot-box did not in fact uphold the theory of the revolution : the home policy of Lamartine's Government had a limited appeal ; there was little in its foreign policy, apart perhaps from some slightly hollow phrases about the liberation of Poland, which could inspire Frenchmen who still had memories of Napoleonic glories ; and within a few months disturbances broke out in Paris which were much greater in extent than those associated with the February revolution. Before the end of 1848 a presidential election brought Louis Napoelon to power. This power was to become very nearly absolute the next year, and its meaning was tersely summed up in the dictum that the name of Napoleon was a programme in itself.

Political commentators have sometimes underestimated the effects of the events of 1848 in France, and it would be misleading to regard the revolution simply as an unsuccessful left-wing movement which was promptly smothered by the powers of reaction. In fact, between the election of Louis Napoleon as President and the restoration of the Empire, such measures as a campaign against slums, the establishment of savings banks, of cheap postage and public telegrams, and laws to prevent cruelty to animals and to facilitate the provision of legal assistance were all introduced. On the other hand, the system of *procureurs-généraux* meant in fact the creation of a powerful secret police ; there were bans on political meetings and a vigorous censorship of the press ; the *coup d'état* of December of 1851 was prepared by the arrest of seventy-eight opposition leaders of the Assembly in one night and consummated by some 27,000 other arrests ; and the referendum, which delegated to the President the right of drawing up the constitution, produced a majority which was sufficiently overwhelming to be suggestive of more modern forms of despotism.

What happened in France had, indeed, much in common with the changes which were taking place at the same time in other European countries. The revolution of the intellectuals rather naturally failed in its primary object of introducing a liberal, constitutional form of government, for liberalism is a way of life which does not normally result from revolution. Nevertheless, the heritage in the form of social legislation which the events of 1848 and the next few years conferred was far from negligible.

GERMANY

Germany between 1848 and 1851 provided an even more revealing picture than France of the difficulties of maintaining stable liberal governments. Revolutions had occurred in a number of German states in 1848, which had been predominantly liberal in character. There were also, it is true, a few working-class insurrections, where the motives were primarily economic. Such were the risings staged by impoverished weavers in Silesia as early as 1844, and the peasant risings which occurred in areas where there were considerable numbers of Poles.

In general, however, the revolutions, if such they can be called, were set in motion by intellectuals, and in spite of the appearance of barricades in Berlin there was relatively little bloodshed. A number of petty princes were petitioned for constitutions and obliged by granting them ; the lead to most other states was given by Baden, which had become a refuge for displaced foreign intellectuals, particularly from France ; and a fairly representative temporary government of the period was the one, consisting largely of professors, which was set up in Saxony.

Most of the hopes of the German liberals were, however, centred in the National Assembly established in Frankfort. In this figures of the cultural eminence of Jakob Grimm and Ludwig Uhland participated. Those associated with the Assembly achieved work of considerable academic interest in the drawing up of constitutions, a task for which the Assembly's many lawyers and historians were peculiarly well fitted. The Dahlmann Constitution, providing for a German two-chamber parliament and a hereditary sovereign, had indeed much in common with a blueprint for a German constitution which had been drawn up by the English Prince Consort.

The Frankfort National Assembly, however, suffered from one

*The hopes of the German liberals were centred in the
National Assembly in Frankfort*

disastrous weakness, a weakness which was to wreck a number of organisations in later ages which attempted to transcend national and dynastic barriers ; it disposed of no forces which could be physically effective in ensuring that its decisions were carried out. At one time members of the Assembly were themselves subjected to physical assault by extremist groups in Frankfort ; the elections of 1850 showed that those states which did not wish to return members to the Assembly were not compelled to do so ; and by 1851 the dissolution of the German union, which had never been truly effected, was complete. The Frankfort National Assembly disintegrated because of that condition of human society, which makes the efficacy of laws dependent on force, and because of the triumph of separatism or federalism over German nationalism.

In 1851 German nationalism was, it is true, a force of some consequence, and it found expression in many places besides the Frankfort Assembly. In Potsdam, for instance, a society was formed in 1849 for eradicating from the German language all words adopted from French or other tongues, in order to " exterminate this brand of slavery which for centuries has rested on the glorious mother tongue." In 1851 Engels, writing to Marx from Manchester, put forward both an old and a new German nationalist policy for Eastern Europe with the words : " Take away from the Poles in the West as much as possible ; under pretext of defence, garrison their fortresses with Germans, let them make a mess of things for themselves, send them into the fire, eat up their land, palm them off with promises of Riga and Odessa, and if the Russians can be got to move, form an alliance with them, and force the Poles to give in." The line of thought which led from Frederick the Great and the Empress Catherine to Ribbentrop and Molotov had a number of distinguished advocates.

Nevertheless, German nationalist feeling was not strong enough to bring into being a single German state. The German princes, many of whom were popular with their subjects, managed in general to retain the right to divide Germany according to dynastic principles ; the Hanse towns, among other small states, were dissuaded by economic considerations from joining the union known as the Zollverein ; and the strength and influence of Prussia served to hinder—not, as later, to assist—the achievement of German unity.

The years 1850 and 1851 were years in which Prussia suffered a number of serious setbacks. There was one setback over a crisis in Hesse-Cassel, which had threatened to lead to a European war ; another in the outcome of the war with Denmark over Schleswig-Holstein ; and what may well be regarded as a third in the terms of a secret treaty which was concluded with Austria in 1851. However, in spite of these setbacks, Prussia remained the strongest of the purely German states. This made the influence which she exerted against the project for a united Germany of paramount importance. The curiously ineffective Prussian monarch, Frederick William, refused the crown offered by the Frankfort Assembly, and in 1851 Bismarck, who began his political career in a movement largely concerned with maintaining the independent identity of Prussia, became Prussian delegate to the traditional Diet of the German Confederation.

The German liberals, therefore, contemplating the state of Germany in 1851, were bound to feel that their efforts had largely resulted in failure. Germany was not a united nation with an enlightened constitution, but a number of loosely connected territories. Nevertheless, much of what was achieved in the stirring years 1848 and 1849 had survived. Many of the princes decided to allow reforms, which they had introduced under pressure, to remain when the threat of insurrection receded. Even in Prussia the constitution of 1849 remained in force. Moreover, the liberals of 1848 achieved another triumph, an intangible but none the less lasting one. This was the creation of a tradition that liberalism and nationalism were not incompatible in Germany. The tradition survived with difficulty ; it was commonly neglected and sometimes distorted into a myth ; but that it had a basis in reality was perhaps more decisively proved in the middle of the nineteenth century than at any other time in German history.

AUSTRIA

In the Austrian Empire the course of events between 1848 and 1851 was in many respects even less satisfactory to the advocates of sweeping changes than it was in Germany. There were two main types of revolutionary movement within the Habsburg dominions. One was primarily concerned with changes in the general social structure ; the other was an expression of the desire of different racial groups within the Empire to gain their national independence. The first type found its main strength in Vienna, the second in the non-Germanic, particularly the Hungarian and Italian territories. By the end of 1851 the old order had gained an evident victory over all these movements, yet certain substantial concessions had been won by its opponents.

In 1848 the system, which Metternich had done so much to create, collapsed with a suddenness comparable with that of the overthrow of the French monarchy. The force which destroyed it could hardly be regarded as a rising of the people. In fact, when the Vienna National Guard was formed in April, 1848, workmen were specifically excluded from it, and in many respects the insurrection was difficult to distinguish from a students' demonstration. However, rulers were being banished elsewhere in Europe, and this particular insurrection was enough to overthrow a suddenly paralysed Government, which had ruled a vast empire for decades. The " insurrection morale," to which Louis-Philippe had referred, was repeated : Metternich fled to England ; the Court was moved from Vienna to Innsbruck, and again later to Olmütz ; and before the end of 1848 the Emperor Ferdinand abdicated.

By the last day of 1851, however, the recovery of the Austrian Government from the shocks of revolution could be said to be complete. On that particular day a plan was announced—again suggestive of an earlier French parallel—for the assumption of absolute power by Ferdinand's successor. This was the young Emperor Francis Joseph, who was to be advised by a nominated imperial council. The so-called Stadion Constitution, which had never really come into force because of the maintenance of emergency powers, was thereby abolished.

The system of Metternich had not been altogether restored. The freeing of the peasants from various feudal burdens proved to be a permanent measure ; Schwarzenberg, who succeeded to the post of Prime Minister, chose a varied assortment of ministers to assist him, including the liberal Count Stadion and the ex-revolutionary Alexander Bach ; and it was in 1851, for instance, that the first trial by jury took place in Vienna. Nevertheless, the Austrian Empire had shown a remarkable power of survival not only against a liberal revolt but also against a variety of powerful nationalist movements.

Of these nationalist movements the most effective was that which occurred in Hungary. War was openly declared between Austria and a temporarily independent Hungary under Kossuth, but in the end the Hungarians were overcome, partly by Austrian troops, and partly by the intervention of troops of other nationalities. The Hungarians had been unwise in neglecting the interests of the other subject races of the Empire. In consequence, they found themselves opposed by powerful Croat forces as well as by Serb levies, and the final blow came when Russian troops were suddenly marched into Hungary in 1849.

Meanwhile a less powerful Czech movement had also been crushed, when Prague, which had temporarily fallen into the hands of insurrectionary forces, was reconquered by Austrian troops. In the Italian provinces of the Empire insurrections had also occurred, but victory in the end was gained by the forces of the Austrian Marshal Radetsky, which for a long period were operating almost independently of the Vienna Government.

The nationalist risings within the Austrian Empire between 1848 and 1851 were not successful. Nevertheless, there was a significance for the future in the holding of the first Slav Congress at Prague in 1848. The delegates were divided into three groups, the Czechoslovak, the Polish-Ruthene and the Illyrian, the last-named shortly changing its name to " Yugoslav." Moreover, a number of Hungarians, including Kossuth, who escaped from Central Europe by way of Turkey, succeeded in having themselves acclaimed in influential circles in the West as the true representatives of an independent Hungary. Kossuth's progress through England in 1851 was that of a triumphant hero—the Great Exhibition having ended, he was for days the central figure in the newspapers—and the British Government acknowledged its sympathy with the revolutionaries by offering to pay £8 to every Hungarian refugee arriving from Turkey who wanted assistance in meeting the cost of his passage to America.

Kossuth

ITALY

In Italy the success of the Austrian armies in the north signified the collapse of a series of revolutionary movements which had occurred in various parts of the country between 1848 and 1851. For a time these revolts had been remarkably successful. Even Pope Pius IX, who had encouraged liberals by his formation of an advisory Council of State, and Italian nationalists by uttering the words " God bless Italy," had been forced to leave Rome and take refuge in Gaeta. Other foreign armies apart from the Austrian, however, intervened against the Italian insurrectionaries. In the end it was the arrival of French troops, who entered Rome after overcoming some resistance organised by Garibaldi, which made possible the Pope's return.

By 1851 the Pope was once again enthroned in Rome ; the Government of Naples, where anarchic conditions had followed the 1848 rising, was suppressing its opponents with that cruelty which so deeply shocked Gladstone ; a small revolt was brewing in Lombardy-Venice, but it was to be put down the next year ; and only in Piedmont, where Cavour became Minister of Finance in 1851, were there encouraging prospects of the creation of a united Italy in conformity with the principles of nineteenth-century liberalism.

SWITZERLAND

In Switzerland, on the other hand, the trend of events was in a rather different direction. A civil war had broken out after the Federal Diet at Berne in 1847 had decided to dissolve the League known as the Sonderbund. This League had been formed by the largely Catholic cantons of Luzern, Uri, Schwyz, Unterwalden, Zug, Fribourg and Valais. The war was to some extent a clash between Catholics and Protestants, and religious issues were among the main causes of dispute. It was not, however, a purely religious war, for no restrictions were placed at its conclusion on the freedom of worship of the losers, and the Sonderbund armies were in fact commanded by a Protestant, Ulrich von Salis-Soglio.

The outcome of the war was a defeat for the Sonderbund and the removal of any separatist threat. After the war the constitution was revised and provided for a federal state in place of a league of states. A permanent capital was established at Berne ; equality before the law and liberty of belief and residence were recognised ; and uniformity of coinage, postal services, weights and measures, and customs was introduced. Although Prussia retained some nominal rights over Neuchatel until 1857, by 1851 the modern structure and constitution of Switzerland had largely been created.

Federal troops entering Fribourg during the Swiss Civil War

BELGIUM AND THE NETHERLANDS

Both Belgium and the Netherlands were directly affected by the various forms of contagion which spread across the greater part of Europe between 1848 and 1851, but in both countries changes were effected peacefully. Belgium had had the advantage of an election in 1847, in which the Liberals had gained a large majority. In consequence the Government could easily adapt itself to the prevailing political mood by introducing electoral reforms which greatly extended the franchise. In the Netherlands, too, a Fundamental Law was promulgated in 1848, setting out the form of a two-chamber parliament ; and although tension between Catholics and Protestants was increasing, the Ministry of the new King, William III, was liberal in character and enjoyed some Catholic support.

SCANDINAVIA

The cause of Scandinavian unity was noticeably advanced around the middle of the century, both in the literary field and by the action of numerous individual Swedes and Norwegians in assisting Denmark in her war over Schleswig-Holstein. In 1849 a Danish constitution providing for a two-chamber parliament and liberty of the press and public meeting was adopted, and in 1850 a temporary settlement was achieved in the protracted and involved Schleswig-Holstein dispute. Of the Schleswig-Holstein question Palmerston in later years was to say that only three people had ever really understood it—" the Prince Consort, who is dead, a German professor, who has gone mad, and I, who have forgotten all about it." Instances of its complexity were afforded by the fact that, for a time, Schleswig was administered by a British as well as a Danish and a Prussian commissioner, and that in 1851 Holstein was policed by Austrian troops.

Sweden and Norway in 1851 were joined in a personal union under one crown. As long as the King had been Charles XIV, the Bernadotte who never mastered the Swedish language, Norwegian politicians had had the satisfaction of dealing regularly with one decisive individual, who was their own King as well as the King of Sweden. Under Oscar I, his successor, however, they found themselves more and more often confronted with Swedish officials, an arrangement which led to growing Norwegian resentment.

In the foreign policy of the two countries, from whose day-to-day conduct Norwegians were virtually excluded, the close friendship with Russia, to which Charles XIV had strenuously adhered, steadily diminished, and the movement advocating the liberation of Finland from Russian rule—a movement which was to become even more popular when the Crimean War broke out—was already gathering strength. In home affairs, in spite of some street riots in Stockholm in 1848, the period was one of relative calm in comparison with what was occurring elsewhere in Europe. The major acts of legislation in one country or the other around the middle of the century were those concerned with reform of the marriage laws, the spread of free trade, the more benevolent treatment of the insane, and measures to cope with a problem which has long concerned Swedish politicians, the problem of alcoholism.

SPAIN AND PORTUGAL

In Spain the year 1851 was distinguished by the triumph of the extreme clerical party. One dictatorial figure, Narvaez, was overthrown by another, Murillo, who dissolved the Cortes, put through financial legislation by decree and concluded a Concordat. In Portugal, where a rebellion had ended in 1847 with the surrender of the rebels to British troops, a new revolt had broken out in 1851, which proved successful and which initiated the period of moderate reform associated with Saldanha. Portugal thus provided a case in which the British, contrary to their normal practice under Palmerston's direction, intervened actively against rebel forces.

RUSSIA

During the years of disturbance from 1848 to 1851 the powers in the councils of Europe which were least affected by the prevailing moods of the time were those with predominantly Asiatic territories. Even in the dependencies and former dependencies of these powers the revolutionary movements were less vigorous than in other parts of Europe.

Russia, for instance, in the middle of the century was passing through a dark age. A number of peasant risings occurred annually, but no progress towards the emancipation of the serfs was achieved, although the outright sale of serfs had by then been forbidden. Some of the measures taken in Russia in 1851 and in the immediately preceding years included the incorporation of an enactment against strikes in the criminal code ;   a decree forbidding newspapers to comment favourably on scientific inventions until they had been officially pronounced sound ; and the setting up of a committee of musical experts to discover whether there was any likelihood that musical notes might be used as ciphers. There were indications of increased industrialisation in Russia, such as the completion of the St. Petersburg-Moscow railway in 1851, the opening up of the port of Nicholaievsk, and a great expansion in the cotton industry. In the matter of Government expenditure, however, the outstanding development was a large and steady expansion of the armed forces, an expansion which was to prove of value when the Crimean War broke out.

POLAND

Even in the most turbulent part of the Russian Empire, Poland, the middle of the century was a period of relative calm, the year 1848 falling nearly half-way between the two great Polish risings of the nineteenth century. In those parts of historic Poland under the rule of Austria and Prussia, and also outside Poland, Poles were continually active in insurrectionary movements. There was a strong independence movement in the province of Poznań, and in 1848 there were demonstrations in Lwów ; the Hungarian Committee of National Defence chose as commanders in the war against Austria the Poles, Bem and Dembicki, and Miero-slawski was one of the leaders of the Baden insurrection. In a number of European conservative circles, indeed, the name " Pole " was held to be virtually synonymous with " revolutionary," but within the Russian Empire the consequences of the risings of the early thirties were still too strongly felt for any concerted Polish action to be effective. The period was in fact one of the many in which Poles were confronted with the conflicting magnetisms of their own soil and freedom to organise in exile. The Polish intellectual capital at the time was Paris, but numerous Poles were emigrating to America. However, the so-called extreme Polish democratic party, with a certain spirit of contradiction, advised Poles not to take advantage of the offer of £8 towards their passage money which the British Government offered to Polish as well as to Hungarian refugees who had escaped through Turkey.

TURKEY

The propping up of the Turkish Empire was the continual concern of a number of European politicians occupied with the problem of maintaining the balance of power in Europe and the Near East around the middle of the century. Events were to prove that their anxieties about a Turkish collapse were not altogether justified. The Sultan Abdul Mejid maintained in a rather more easy-going manner the tradition of his father, Mahmoud II, who had been something of a westerniser, and who had liquidated the Janissaries as well as a number of enviable official posts, such as those of the Keeper of the Nightingales and Keeper of the Heron's Plumes. Under the rule of Abdul Mejid, at whose court the British Ambassador, Stratford Canning, a pronounced Russophobe, enjoyed an almost unique advisory power, the inequalities before the law from which non-Moslem subjects of the Empire had suffered were removed ; a Council of State and a State Bank were instituted ; and in theory the farming of taxes was brought to an end, although there were considerable differences between theory and practice in Turkish administration.

In the Arab lands of the Turkish Empire the foundations of the Arab national movement were being laid in the literary and academic field. The Society of Arts and Sciences was founded at Beirut in 1847, and the Oriental Society, sponsored by the Jesuits, in 1850. In the political field, however, Arab unity was still only a dream. When the Turks, after the Egyptian evacuation of Syria, established a new administrative regime dividing the Lebanon into two districts—the one mainly Moslem and the other mainly Christian—the effect was to increase the hostility between Maronites and Druzes. This hostility, which was to culminate later in a series of massacres, was consistently fanned by British support of the Druzes and French support of the Maronites.

SERBIA AND GREECE

In the European lands which had recently secured freedom from Turkish rule, Serbia enjoyed a period of comparative peace under Alexander Karageorgevitch, the son of the famous liberator. There was growing resentment at Karageorgevitch's refusal to summon the National Assembly, but it was a prudent omission from his own point of view, for one of the first steps the Assembly was to take when it did meet was the passing of a resolution insisting on his dethronement. In Greece the period of absolute rule by the Bavarian King Otto had been brought to an end by a military revolt in 1843, and the main political cleavage was between the so-called French or Russian party on the one hand and the so-called English party on the other. The French or Russian party on the whole received the support of the King, and its opponents the support of two separate demonstrations by British naval forces within four years.

CHINA

In the Far East the process of opening up huge new territories to Western economic and political activity advanced with a new rapidity in the middle of the century, a process which was to lead to the establishment in 1853 of the Shanghai International Settlement. The British led the United States and the other European nations in winning concessions from the Chinese. They concluded first the Nanking Treaty, which ceded Hong Kong to the British Crown and opened up what were to be known as the treaty ports to British commerce ; and later they concluded a second treaty, which made British citizens in certain areas subject to British and not Chinese judicial authority. In the interior of China in 1851 there was a major rebellion led by Hung-Siu-Tsuen, whose followers, known as the Taipings, two years later captured Nanking.

Commodore Perry being received by the Imperial Japanese Commissioners

JAPAN

In Japan a comparable penetration by Western influences had not yet occurred by 1851, although the United States Government had already begun to make the overtures which were to lead to Commodore Perry's expedition two years later. The ancient Japanese social structure, at the head of which stood the distant figure of the Mikado, while the real power was exercised by the Shogun, still survived in a country strangely immune from foreign influence. It was, however, to collapse with extraordinary rapidity once foreign penetration had taken effect.

SOUTH AMERICA

In South America in the middle of the century, a number of countries which had recently passed out of the colonial stage were developing independent nationhoods. There were some striking differences between the ways in which this process was forwarded in Portuguese and in Spanish America. In Brazil, which had not been subjected to the activities of the liberators, Bolívar and San Martín, a hereditary Empire was maintained, although the break with Portugal was complete. Possibly as a result of the orderly progression from the colonial to the independent stage, the country enjoyed internal peace around the middle of the century, and an ancient culture, essentially Portuguese but subjected to strong French influence, was maintained with some vigour. The two principal Brazilian parties, the Conservatives and the Liberals, agreed to the retention of considerable powers by the Emperor Pedro, but an important concession to contemporary liberal feeling was made in the abolition of the slave trade. By 1851 this trade had very nearly come to an end.

In the countries of Spanish America, from Venezuela, where the liberation movement had had its origins, to Peru, whose people, Bolívar had stated, had had to be liberated in spite of themselves, the period was one of sporadic disturbances. Power was generally exercised by military dictators, a number of whom were mestizos. The main political issue was at least nominally that of centralisation or decentralisation of rule, but it was generally obscured by personal considerations.

One of the most personally successful dictators was Juan Manuel de Rosas, who by 1851 had ruled in the Argentine Confederation despotically for more than twenty years, apart from a short interruption during which he had lost power. Under his rule a stable settlement with the Indians was achieved ; there was a huge increase in cattle-breeding ; and a peace was concluded with the British in 1849 after a period of trade disputes and blockade. On the other hand, the country came more and more under the control of a powerful secret police ; a general obligation to wear the red ribbon of the Federalists was instituted ; and Rosas's personal cruelty was notorious. In 1851 Rosas was overthrown as a result of a rising which enjoyed some Brazilian and Paraguayan support. Like so many other displaced leaders of the period, he chose England as his country of refuge, and he subsequently spent a number of peaceful years farming in the neighbourhood of Southampton.

*　　　　*　　　　*

In every one of the countries whose political background at the time has been briefly outlined, Britain a hundred years ago felt a direct interest. The feeling of having both an inherent right and a responsibility to be a world power—a feeling which has subsequently developed in a number of other nations—was already well established in Britain, a fact which contrasts strikingly with the reputation which the British then, as now, enjoyed for being exceptionally insular in their outlook.

During the years immediately preceding the Great Exhibition, British foreign policy was conducted by one of the most vigorous Foreign Secretaries this country has ever produced. Something of a myth has now grown up about the foreign policy of Palmerston, in which that policy is pictured as being bombastic, illogically successful and, in a rather attractive way, unprincipled.

There is a good deal to be said in support of this myth, but it is probably no more than a half-truth. Perhaps the best summing up of Palmerston as a Foreign Secretary was that made by one of his contemporaries, the Duke of Argyll, when he wrote : " Palmerston was not, in the ordinary meaning of the word, an unprincipled politician. He was honest in his purposes, and truthful in his prosecution of them. That ' honesty is the best policy ' was his favourite adage in diplomacy . . . but he had no high ideals for the future of the world, and had a profound distrust of those who professed to be guided by such ideals."

Palmerston had in fact a firm belief in certain moral causes, to whose furtherance he was ready to dedicate British power. One such cause was the campaign against the slave trade, which he prosecuted wherever he had an opportunity. He insisted, for example, that abolition of the slave trade was " a preliminary and indispensable condition " for British recognition of the State of Texas.

He also had a profound belief in what he conceived to be the cause of liberalism. This belief he voiced with exceptional clarity. He once described Miguel of Portugal as " this destroyer of constitutional freedom, this breaker of solemn oaths, this enslaver of his country, this trampler upon public law " ; and on the occasion of Louis-Philippe's accession to the throne he declared his readiness to " drink the cause of Liberalism all over the world." By the middle of the century he had changed his views on the House of Orleans but not on liberal principles. Palmerston's international reputation as a liberal champion was not the least of the causes of a tradition of friendship for Britain which grew up in the middle of the century in a number of countries suffering from oppressive foreign rule. Among such countries were both Hungary and Italy.

Another cause which Palmerston believed must be upheld, even at considerable risk and inconvenience, was that of the inalienable rights of British citizens wherever they might happen to be. One of the most remarkable examples of his belief in this cause was his action in sending a naval squadron to cruise off the coast of Greece to support the claims of the notorious Don Pacifico. Pacifico was a Gibraltar Jew with a deplorable reputation, but none the less a British subject, who considered he was being inadequately compensated by the Greek Government for the fact that his house had been burnt in some anti-Jewish riots. Palmerston's action was highly dangerous and in many respects outrageous, but it is significant that he seldom, and perhaps never, made a better speech than the one, lasting more than four hours, in which he defended his part in the Pacifico affair, and in which he made his memorable comparison of the British and Roman empires with the words, " Civis Romanus sum."

To regard the British foreign policy conducted by Palmerston in the middle of the last century as unprincipled would indeed be an over-simplification. There were, however, abundant reasons for considering it inconsistent, as Palmerston was himself ready to admit. Indeed he even went so far as to denounce what he called the " puerile vanity of consistency." Thus, when the cause of liberalism which he had so much at heart seemed likely to triumph everywhere in Europe in 1848, Palmerston's main concern was the prevention of a war of opinion. This, he feared, might upset the balance of power in Europe, which had been established in 1815, and whose maintenance he had once told a British Ambassador must be the principal aim of British policy.

Palmerston's critics had at one time accused him of having no policy but that of a French alliance, and the principal piece of advice he gave to Lord Malmesbury in 1852 was to " keep well with France." Yet at different times he was prepared publicly to insult France in an electioneering speech, to try to thwart French interests in Belgium and over the question of a suitable husband for the Queen of Spain, and to seek Russian rather than French co-operation in Egyptian affairs.

Lord Palmerston

The danger from Russia was one of which Palmerston was constantly aware, particularly after the intervention of Russian troops in Hungary in 1849. In commenting on Turkish affairs, for instance, he enunciated the dictum that " one must go by the general rules and believe that where Russian agents are employed there must be intrigue on foot." He had earlier summarised Russian aims in Greece as the establishment of " a predominant influence . . . for the purpose of directing the external affairs of Greece in such a manner as to make the policy of that country subservient to Russian objects, and for the purpose of prescribing such a system of management in the internal administration of Greece as might prevent any free or liberal institutions in that country." Yet even with the coming of the Crimean war he was to make it clear to the Poles that there was to be no conflict with Russia " à outrance."

Palmerston was the *bête-noire* of successive Austrian Governments. Metternich had a favourite rhyme which he used to intone and which ran :

> " *Hat der Teufel einen Sohn,*
> *So ist er sicher Palmerston.*"

And when Palmerston was dismissed towards the end of 1851 Schwarzenberg gave a ball in Vienna to celebrate the event. Yet Palmerston echoed with conviction the remark that if the Austrian Empire did not already exist it would have to be invented, and on one occasion he even went so far as to call Austria " the natural ally of England in the East."

It is indeed arguable that the very inconsistencies in the British conduct of foreign affairs did themselves constitute a policy, the policy enunciated in Palmerston's contention that " we have no eternal allies, and we have no perpetual enemies." Palmerston had his difficulties at home as well as overseas. The constant concern with foreign affairs shown by the Court hampered his freedom as a Foreign Secretary, and he was fully aware of the relative defencelessness of Britain and the difficulty of persuading his fellow-countrymen to remedy that weakness. He once stated that steam no longer made the Channel an effective barrier, and that it was " almost as difficult to persuade the people of this country to provide themselves with the means of defence as it would be for them to defend themselves without those means." For these reasons his very tight-rope walking, switches of front and suddenness of decision—practices which all suggest an inclination towards expediency rather than principle—can defensibly be regarded as forming a single policy, that of concurrently preserving peace and Britain's prestige as a world power in every country of the world.

One thing is certain about British foreign policy a hundred years ago, and that is that it was conducted by a man of extraordinary conscientious-ness and zeal. Palmerston was a difficult man to work for, and if sub-mitted to that searching but valuable test, the general opinion of his subordinates, he must be found seriously wanting. Not only did he con-tinually insult and annoy foreign ambassadors, particularly by his unpunctuality, but he was widely disliked by the Foreign Office staff, and he was capable of returning a despatch from a British envoy with the instruction that it should be rewritten in blacker ink. He was certainly a martinet. In his early days at the War Office he had been ruthless in his insistence that papers should be speedily acted on and not lost, the latter solution being one which he had " occasion perpetually to observe." He also made a shrewd comment when he stated that " no climate agrees with a British diplomatist, except that of Paris, Florence and Naples." However, he demanded of himself every bit as much as he demanded of others. He claimed to read every despatch sent to the Foreign Office " down to the least important letter of the lowest vice-consul." At a time when all these despatches were in manuscript and the outgoing despatches from the Foreign Office numbered some 30,000 a year, this was something of an achievement.

To the general British public the particular form of patriotism which Palmerston's foreign policy represented had a wide appeal, and he was an extremely popular figure. His removal from the control of foreign affairs after 1851 was indeed one of the main causes of the unpopularity from which the Prince Consort suffered at that time. There were many qualities in Palmerston's make-up which endeared him to the British public. Like Mr. Winston Churchill, he did not altogether fit into the party machine, and he was commonly thought of as a patriot rather than as a party man ; he accepted without question the responsibility of his class to govern Britain and of Britain to give a lead to all other countries ;

he was known as a sportsman, and, perhaps most important of all, he seemed to grow in stature as he grew in age.

There were, of course, other foreign policies which Britain could and periodically did adopt besides that of Palmerston. There was the rather more cautious policy of Aberdeen, an able statesman who was less prone to risk errors of commission than Palmerston and who, while Guizot was in power, achieved an effective entente with France. There were the restraints imposed on Palmerston by the Prince Consort, whose understanding of German affairs was profound—whereas Palmerston's was curiously lacking—who was just as conscientious as Palmerston in assembling facts, and who was found far easier to deal with by foreign dignitaries. There was also the pacifist foreign policy of Cobden, which was never really put into effect.

Palmerston, too, was periodically out of power. He suffered one of his eclipses in December, 1851, when he finally overstrained the patience of the Prime Minister. For some months Russell had had reason to find Palmerston's public actions trying. There had been one occasion on which Palmerston had barely apologised when the Austrian General Haynau had been attacked by the employees of Barclay and Perkins's brewery ; another occasion on which Palmerston, after agreeing not to receive Kossuth at his home, had accepted addresses from Islington and Finsbury, in which the Austrian and Russian Emperors were described as " odious and detestable tyrants " ; and the final clash came when Palmerston, without consulting the Court or the Cabinet, expressed approval of Louis Napoleon's *coup d'état*. After this last incident Palmerston's departure from the Foreign Office was inevitable.

Nevertheless, during the five years preceding the Great Exhibition, British foreign policy was before all else the policy of Palmerston. It was a policy which can easily be criticised, and those who decry it usually argue that it could have succeeded only in a period of British commercial and maritime supremacy. However, it was during just such a period that this policy was put into effect, and not the least remarkable of its features was the fact that it succeeded to the extent it did without the support of either a large or an efficient army.

When Palmerston was at the Foreign Office in the years leading up to the Great Exhibition, the land defences of Britain consisted in the first instance of some forty field-guns and siege-guns, whose carriages were for the most part unserviceable. At least two-thirds of the regiments of the Army were regularly stationed in the colonies, and of the rest the majority were needed to maintain order in Ireland. In 1847 the Army Reserve was found to number only 1,600 men, and a few years earlier a Bill had had to be introduced into Parliament to enable the Government to call upon the Chelsea Pensioners to assist the civil power in maintaining order.

The British soldier was, moreover, an object of contempt to his compatriots. Still subjected to the disciplinary measure of flogging at a time when it had been abandoned in most other civilised countries ; housed in barracks in which even as late as 1849 typhus epidemics raged ; given his last meal of the day shortly after noon ; offered virtually no incentive —when a soldier was promoted to the rank of sergeant, for instance, he lost his good conduct pay—and exiled for years to unhealthy climates with hardly any protection against tropical diseases ; he was regarded, with some justification, as belonging to the lowest stratum of the population. Some improvements in the soldier's lot were indeed effected in the forties. The Government gave official sanction to the institution of regimental savings banks and libraries, and a number of barracks were made less insanitary. However, it was not until the next decade, with the coming of the Crimean War, that the people of Britain became generally aware of the inefficiency of their Army and of the neglect from which their soldiers suffered. Then it was learnt that the troops who were to besiege Sevastopol were landed without any wagons or draught animals, and it needed the energy and courage of a Florence Nightingale to ensure that even primitive forms of medical care were available.

It is true that it was to the Navy and not to the Army that the British people looked for their first line of defence. However, in the middle of the century there was no regular Navy in the sense in which the term is understood to-day. Except for a certain number of men who were trained in gunnery and were given a seven-year contract, the ratings on Her Majesty's ships were simply hired and discharged as and when they were required. The bulk of them came from those members of the poorest classes in the dockyard towns who could find no other employment. Among the officers, too, there was little regular active employment, and at any moment the great majority of naval officers were to be found idle on shore and entitled to only a proportion of the full pay of their rank. Even in the technical field the backwardness of the Navy was remarkable. In 1851 a naval spokesman stated in a public lecture that " iron does not appear to be applicable for ships of war."

Such being the condition of the British forces, it cannot be seriously argued that Palmerston's foreign policy was rendered possible by any preponderance of armed strength. It is true that Britain did enjoy a position of supremacy in the commercial field, and her greatness in the middle of the last century was no doubt due to her wealth rather than to Palmerston's conduct of foreign affairs. It was, however, Palmerston's constant endeavour to make the best use possible of the power which that wealth conferred. That he was successful in following the course which he set himself there is ample evidence. There were indeed cogent reasons other than purely economic ones why in 1851 such an event as the Great Exhibition should take place in London and not in any other city of the world.

CHAPTER EIGHT

EVENTS OF THE YEAR 1851

POLITICAL EVENTS IN BRITAIN IN 1851

IN THE year of the Great Exhibition the Prime Minister was Lord John Russell. The Government was defeated in the course of the year over the County Franchise Bill, but as no other Government was formed Russell continued in office. Lord Palmerston was dismissed from the Foreign Office after expressing approval of Louis Napoleon's *coup d'état* without consulting the Court or the Cabinet. Lord Ashley, who in the same year also had his fiftieth birthday and succeeded to the Earldom of Shaftesbury, introduced a Bill to encourage the establishment of lodging-houses for the working classes. The window-tax was repealed. Disraeli's motion calling on the Government to introduce without delay measures for the relief of owners and occupiers of land was defeated by fourteen votes. An Act was passed giving the Crown power to enclose and plant 10,000 acres in the New Forest. Bronterre O'Brien founded the National Reform League, which advocated State purchase of land for leasing to the unemployed. Kossuth arrived in England.

ECCLESIASTICAL EVENTS

Following numerous petitions against " papal agression " and some anti-Catholic rioting, an Act was passed which declared the ecclesiastical titles conferred by the Pope in Britain to be illegal. Manning was received into the Roman Catholic Church, having previously resigned the archdeaconry of Chichester. An ecclesiastical census was taken, which showed that some ten million persons could be seated in places of worship, of which just over half were Anglican. Newman, who also had his fiftieth birthday in that year, delivered lectures on the position of Catholics in England in the Birmingham Corn Exchange. A new plot of ground was obtained for building a Catholic Cathedral in Westminster.

The landing-point of the submarine cable near Calais

SCIENTIFIC AND ENGINEERING EVENTS

The first successful submarine cable to Calais was laid. Scott Archer revolutionised the practice of photography by making known his wet plate collodion process. Donisthorpe and Lister perfected their wool-combing machine. The Royal School of Mines was founded. Branches of the engineering trade united in the Amalgamated Society of Engineers.

LITERARY EVENTS

A treaty was signed between Britain and France for the suppression of literary piracy. *Cranford* began to appear in serial form in Dickens's magazine, *Household Words*. George Borrow published *Lavengro*. Tennyson wrote his *Dedication* to Queen Victoria, in which he summed up the contemporary scene by stating that " her court was pure ; her life serene ; God gave her peace ; her land reposed." Thackeray delivered a series of lectures on English humorists of the eighteenth century. Elizabeth Barrett Browning published *Casa Guidi Windows*. Disraeli published his biography of Lord George Bentinck. Trollope made a tour of the west country, thereby acquiring his first contact with Barchester.

THEATRICAL AND ARTISTIC EVENTS

Landseer painted *The Monarch of the Glens*. Millais painted *Mariana of the Moated Grange*. Holman Hunt painted *The Hireling Shepherd*. Ruskin published an essay in which he came forward as a champion of the pre-Raphaelites. T. W. Robertson's first play, *A Night's Adventure*, was produced at the Olympic theatre but was little noticed. Douglas Jerrold's *Black-Eyed Susan* was revived with success. Macready made his last stage appearace, playing the part of Macbeth with, as he put it, " a reality, a vigour, a truth, a dignity that I never before threw into my delineation of this favourite character."

ARCHITECTURAL EVENTS

The Marble Arch was moved to its present site from its former position in front of Buckingham Palace. Ruskin published the first volume of his *Stones of Venice*, which included his famous chapter on the nature of Gothic. Holloway Prison, Colney Hatch Lunatic Asylum, and the Army and Navy Club were completed. The Record Office in Chancery Lane and the new building for King's Cross Station were begun.

COLONIAL EVENTS

Gold was discovered at Ballarat. Livingstone reached the Zambesi. Search was continued for Sir John Franklin's expedition, which had disappeared in search of the north-west passage from the Atlantic to the Pacific. In Parliament Sir William Molesworth moved for an address praying for the discontinuance of transportation to Van Diemen's Land.

Sir J. Hawsley's Teddington, winner of the 1851 Derby

SPORTING EVENTS

The Derby was won by Sir J. Hawsley's Teddington, a 3-1 favourite ridden by J. Marson. The Grand National was won by Mr. Osborne's Abd-el-Kader, ridden by T. Abbott. Cambridge beat Oxford at cricket

J. M. W. Turner, died 1851

in the only sporting contest between the universities that year by an innings and four runs ; the Players beat the Gentlemen by an innings and twenty-two ; and England beat Kent by eight wickets, largely owing to an excellent all-round performance by Wisden.

OBITUARY

Of those who died in the year of the Great Exhibition the figure best known to posterity was the painter, J. M. W. Turner. The deaths also occurred in that year of William Adams, who had been one of the three plenipotentiaries sent to conclude the 1815 Convention of Commerce with the United States ; Joanna Baillie, the Scottish dramatist and poetess; William Clowes, the co-founder of the Primitive Methodists, who was also a Staffordshire potter and a champion dancer ; James Crabb, who conducted a mission to convert the Gipsies of the New Forest ; David Dyce-Sombre, whose father had been Satrap of Sirdhana in Bengal under the Mogul Emperor, and who was himself returned as M.P. for Sudbury, only to be later unseated for bribery and then pronounced of unsound mind ; the son of George III, who was known in England as the Duke of Cumberland, and who succeeded to the throne of Hanover as Ernest Augustus ; Allen Gardiner, a missionary in both Zululand and Patagonia, who eventually died of starvation in Tierra del Fuego ; William Hodgson, who died at the age of 106, and who had been imprisoned for making a revolutionary speech in 1793 ; James Johnston, who in 1823 had put forward a plan for establishing steam communication with India via the Mediterranean and the Red Sea ; Gentleman Jones, the actor; the third Earl of Liverpool, who had volunteered for the Austrian Army at Austerlitz, and who later became British Under-Secretary for War ; Henry Marshall, who instituted the keeping of medical statistics in the Army ; William Martin, one of three remarkable brothers, of whom one was confined in an asylum for threatening to shoot the Bishop of Oxford, and another was a well-known painter specialising in such subjects as the fall of Babylon, William himself being best known for his publication, *A Challenge to the Whole Terrestrial Globe*, in which he announced the discovery of perpetual motion and the collapse of Newtonism ; Joshua

Ernest Augustus of Hanover, died 1851

Milne, an actuary to the Sun Life Assurance Society, whose *Treatise on the Valuation of Annuities* revolutionised actuarial science ; Joseph Moore, a wealthy button manufacturer from Birmingham, who was said to have induced Mendelssohn to compose the *Elijah* ; Charles Palmer, a major-general who had served with distinction in the Peninsular War and then became proprietor of the Bath theatre ; Sir Charles Pepys, later Earl of Cottenham, who was Lord Chancellor under Lord John Russell ; Richard Phillips, who discovered the true nature of uranite ; General Sir Roger Sheaffe, who was born in Boston and commanded the British troops at the defence of the town then known as York and now known as Toronto ; Richard Sheil, the Irish dramatist and politician ; Shelley's second wife, whose own best known work was *Frankenstein* ; Thomas Winter, famous as a pugilist under the name of Tom Spring, who, after claiming the boxing championship of England, retired to keep the Castle Tavern in Holborn ; the thirteenth Earl of Derby, a President of the Linnean and Zoological Societies, who presented a museum to Liverpool ; and Henry Tucker, who overcame the setback of having to serve a prison sentence for attempted rape and was eventually appointed Chairman of the East India Company.

BIRTHS

Among those who were born in 1851 were Sir Horace Avory, the learned judge, who sentenced the murderers of P.C. Gutteridge in 1927 ; Dame Henrietta Barnett, the social reformer, who founded the Hampstead Garden Suburb Trust ; A. C. Bradley, the Shakespearian critic ; Philip Cardew, who invented the voltmeter and the vibratory transmitter for telegraphy ; John Dillon, the Irish nationalist politician ; the fourth Earl Grey, a Governor-General of Canada ; Lord Harris, who in 1880 captained England in the first Test match to be played against Australia in England, and who later became Governor of Bengal ; Bishop Hoare of Hong Kong, who was drowned in Castle Peak Bay while on a preaching tour ; Henry Arthur Jones, the dramatist ; the first Viscount Leverhulme, who founded Lever Brothers and Port Sunlight ; Sir George Newnes, founder of the publishing house and of *Tit-Bits*, the *Strand*, and the

Sir Oliver Lodge, born 1851

Mrs. Humphry Ward, born 1851

Westminster Gazette ; Sir Oliver Lodge, the physicist, who became famous for his work in the field of psychical research ; Francis Paget, Bishop of Oxford ; George Palmer, the founder of Huntley and Palmer's ; Sir Herbert Risley, the anthropologist ; Sir Arthur Schuster, the mathematical physicist, who obtained the first photograph of the spectrum of the solar corona ; Frederick Selous, the hunter and explorer ; Sir Leslie Ward, best known as the cartoonist " Spy " of *Vanity Fair* ; Mrs. Humphry Ward, the novelist from Tasmania ; William Wilson, the astronomer ; and Sir George Younger, who organised the coupon election campaign in 1918.

MISCELLANEOUS EVENTS

The summer of 1851 was a cold and wet one, with mean temperatures from May to August more than two degrees below the average for the preceding twenty-five years. A census was taken which showed that the population of " Great Britain and the islands in the British seas " was 20,959,477, the figure for England and Wales being 17,927,609 and that for Scotland 2,888,742. Bankruptcies numbered 1,381. Mrs. Bloomer made a lecture tour of England advocating the wearing of pantaloons by women. Owens College, Manchester, was founded. Oscar Wilde's parents were married. A murder trial which caused some sensation was that of Thomas Bare, who killed his wife by stabbing her with a triangular saw file.

Part Three

THE
EXHIBITION OF 1851

CHAPTER NINE

PRINCE ALBERT, THE CREATOR
OF THE EXHIBITION

THE real creator of the Great Exhibition was beyond any doubt Prince Albert, who was later to be accorded the title of Prince Consort. Who first thought of the idea of such an exhibition is a question which has been debated, as the origin of any idea always may be. There is certainly a strong case for stating, as the historian of the Crystal Palace, Christopher Hobhouse, did, that the idea originated with Henry Cole, an Assistant Keeper at the Record Office ; and Cole indeed played an important part in the genesis of the scheme. On the other hand, there is evidence that the Prince had been contemplating a project of this nature even before Cole approached him to discuss his own plans.

In any case, once he had decided that the project could and should be put into practice, the Prince worked unreservedly for its success. It was he who suggested a site in Hyde Park in preference to the use of Somerset House for staging the Exhibition ; and of his work as President of the Royal Commission, which was the controlling body, it can be said that, although the other commissioners included men of such distinction as Gladstone, Lord John Russell, Cobden, Henry Labouchère, Lord Stanley, Lord Granville and Sir Charles Lyell, none concerned himself so intimately with the details of the work as the Prince, and none showed in this respect a comparable administrative ability. Yet when the Exhibition was finally closed down, the Prince was still barely thirty-two years of age.

The public readily recognised the Exhibition as the Prince's creation. It was to him that opponents of the scheme directed abusive letters, complaining that he was a German and a revolutionary and was bringing England to destruction ; and when the enormous success of the enterprise became apparent he gained a new popular respect. For posterity, too, his association with the Exhibition has been perpetuated, both by the site chosen for his best known memorial and by the decision to depict him in that extraordinary structure with the catalogue of the Exhibition in his hand.

The character of the Prince Consort is one around which something of a legend has grown up. There is a popular picture of him which is accepted by most people who have a cursory knowledge of the facts of his life, and it is not an attractive one. Indeed few people to-day think of the Prince Consort as an attractive person, yet anyone who troubles to re-examine what is now known of his life will find how remarkably at variance most of it is with the popular picture of him which still prevails.

The Prince Consort of popular tradition was an industrious, worthy, humourless German, on whom the Queen lavished an excess of inexplicable affection. Like Alice's White King, he was continually writing memoranda, for which he had not even the White King's excuse of a defective memory ; the record of his personal virtue was perpetuated in his widow's phrase, " the lily of a blameless life," and the vigour with which she underlined the word " good " in her diary ; his famous memorial and the concert-hall bearing his name remain as reminders of the pretentiousness of which the English nineteenth century was capable, while the unfairness of blaming a man for his own memorial is seldom considered ; his very Christian name has suffered such an unfortunate eclipse that it would to-day need a brave novelist to confer on it a hero and expect to arouse sympathy ; and while the absence of any record of deviations from fidelity on his part have helped to preclude him from popular endearment, he also failed to live to a ripe old age, which in England, in his exalted position, would almost automatically have qualified him for reverence. Finally, he was a German, an accident of birth which made it easy for him to be respected but much less easy for him to be liked in the country of his adoption.

It is true that the task of reassessing the Prince Consort's character has already been undertaken by a number of seekers after truth. It was begun some time ago by Lytton Strachey, who showed how the less

Prince Albert in 1851

attractive features of the Albert of tradition were largely shaped by the eulogies which his widow misguidedly believed should be heaped on his memory ; and his latest and perhaps best biographer, Mr. Roger Fulford, has redressed the balance even further. Nevertheless, the Albert of tradition survives as a strangely misunderstood character.

There is indeed no case for regarding the Prince Consort as a man of startling or picturesque vices. Yet he had certain tastes, which may be regarded as foibles, and which seem oddly at variance with the central figure in the bizarre memorial whom millions of people have contemplated without sympathy. In his university days, for instance, he had been regarded as an accomplished mimic, and he continued to indulge this taste in the English Royal Family circle. A talent for mimicry is one which in most people proceeds from a subtle, appreciative and probably sympathetic humour, and there are good grounds for assuming that in the Prince Consort it proceeded from the same cause. He appears, too, to have enjoyed playing hide-and-seek and flying kites with his children, and he certainly enjoyed playing skittles and billiards with Baron Stockmar. He had a taste for whisky, and, contrary to a belief which was prevalent in his lifetime that he was no sportsman, he shot excellently, could ride well to hounds, and was an exceptionally skilful skater and fencer. Moreover, his very piety was something of which exaggerated notions have been formed. He carried out his religious duties in the manner and with the belief which the age demanded, but theology seems to have been one of the very few subjects of intellectual study which he really found boring.

More significantly, his virtues were not those of a prig. They were those of a man of both unusual intelligence and unusual magnanimity. To this the comments of contemporary men of judgment bear a cumulative testimony which can hardly be neglected. The Duke of Argyll, for instance, both a good observer of men and a good commentator, writing in his memoirs of the Prince Consort, described his " calm, penetrating eye, where moments of reflection were interchanged with glances which bespoke the frequent suggestion of humour and amusement." Lord Ashley gave another facet to the same picture when he described him as " hearty, kind, zealous, sensible."

Numerous unsolicited tributes were also paid to his intelligence and

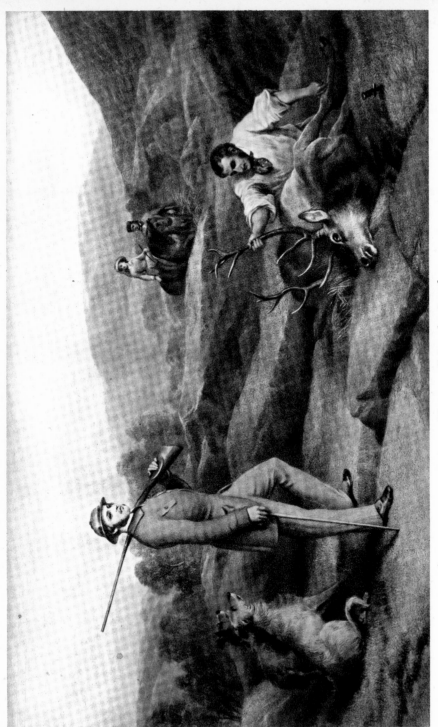

Prince Albert stalking, by Landseer

general ability. Louis Napoleon declared that he had never met his equal. Greville, by no means always a charitable observer, gained the immediate impression that Prince Albert was " very intelligent and highly cultivated." Lord Granville, who held the post of Foreign Secretary, stated that " there is not a Department of the Government regarding all the details and management of which he is not much better informed and more capable than the Minister at the head of it." And even Disraeli, whom the Prince Consort valued so little that he declared him to be lacking in any of the qualities of a gentleman, described the Prince Consort by contrast as " I think the best-educated man I have ever met."

The comments of these different persons, most of whom knew the Prince Consort chiefly in some professional capacity, might carry less weight if they were not confirmed by the opinions of those who lived in the closest relationships with him : his wife, his children, his relatives, his personal advisers and personal servants. Queen Victoria was not only deeply in love with her husband ; her respect for his qualities also grew steadily from year to year. In the early days of their marriage she showed some unwillingness to consult him on affairs of State ; gradually, however, she became more and more dependent on his advice, and after his death she based her conduct largely on what may or may not have been a correct interpretation of what he would have considered right.

Their children also had a deep affection for the Prince. This was particularly strong in the case of their eldest daughter, who was to become the mother of the German Emperor, William II. However, it was also shown by a person so unlike his father as the future King Edward VII., who certainly felt a deeper and more lasting affection for his father than he did for his mother. Among his tenants, too, the Prince Consort was known for his exceptional consideration, and his confidential secretary, George Anson, and his valets were deeply devoted to him.

The evidence of those best qualified to judge being so much at variance with the popular tradition, it is not easy to form a clear picture of the Prince Consort as he was, and the task is made more difficult by the fact that his character was certainly a complex one. Of one of his qualities there can be no question, and that was his exceptional mental capacity. The level of intelligence which he introduced to that branch of the family into which he married was quite a new one. Queen Victoria was a woman with vitality, determination and considerable ability. She had a quick mind, and she was a gifted linguist. Her general intelligence was, however, much inferior to that of her husband.

It would indeed be fair to describe the Prince Consort as an intellectual, for he took a constant and active pleasure in the exercise of his mental faculties. As a student he had been keenly interested in higher mathematics ; he set about the task of understanding England by making a study of constitutional law ; and in the early days of his marriage he found the triviality of social conversation at Court irksome.

Osborne House

However, there was nothing arid about his intellectuality, and the diversity of his serious interests was remarkable. Mr. Fulford, for instance, suggests that the role for which he was ideally equipped was that of a patron of the arts. He composed songs, played the organ and painted, and although he made no claim to be a creative artist of distinction, he believed that his own efforts helped him to understand the work of others —a belief which was justified by the discrimination he showed in the selection of paintings and by Sterndale Bennett's assertion that he was " the ideal amateur of music." He had a particular interest in the physical sciences and a ready understanding of the principles of machinery. He was a painstaking farmer and stockbreeder, and he delighted in interior decoration and the laying out of gardens. In the political field the tribute paid to him by Lord Granville was not unmerited, and in broader social activities he even won the admiration of the exacting Lord Ashley.

He was indeed a man who undertook hard work and the patient study of a subject with readiness. He wrote his numerous memoranda with care and precision, and he kept scrupulously up to date with his correspondence. It would not be true to say that he did not know how to relax ; he did, and he took a special delight, for instance, in walking in mountain scenery. However, he was an intellectual in an age in which frivolity was hardly regarded as a virtue, and in which to be an intellectual was a serious affair. To us who live in the middle of the twentieth century and have known modern educational methods, the programme of learning which he set out for his children—and particularly for the future King Edward VII, who did not take easily to academic discipline—seems not a little alarming. Yet it was not out of keeping with the ideals of the age, and it was certainly drawn up with love and hope and not with harshness.

There was, moreover, nothing petty in the Prince Consort's character. He was deeply affected, for instance, by the political differences which he and the Queen had with Palmerston and by the public reaction to what was known of these differences. About the time of the Great Exhibition he could describe Palmerston as " the man who embittered our whole life." Yet, as the mutual respect between Palmerston and the Prince Consort grew, and as the national threat which the Crimean War represented developed, both men showed sufficient magnanimity to overcome differences which had been profound.

An element of greatness was also evident in the Prince's approach to the peculiar problem of being the Consort of a most determined woman who was passionately in love with him. One method of approach was set out in his memorandum on the duties of a Consort, in which he wrote that " the husband should entirely sink his *own individual* existence in that of his wife—that he should aim at no power by himself or for himself—should shun all ostentation—assume no separate responsibility before the public." Another lay in the extraordinary consideration he showed as a husband, his patience whenever his wife chose to sulk, and

The Royal Family Christmas

the gradual and persuasive exercise of his greater intelligence and greater breadth of mind.

Nevertheless, with all these excellent characteristics, the Prince Consort remained to many people a somewhat distant figure. An observant comment which may help to explain why he did so, was once made by Anson, who remarked on the Prince's " constitutional timidity," a phrase which can be simply interpreted as meaning shyness.

There were also circumstances in the Prince's life in England which might have made another man embittered. They did not have this effect on him, but they may well have increased his tendency to reserve. The transference from Saxe-Coburg, a principality of some 60,000 inhabitants, where royalty was not an excessively exacting status, to the position of Consort of the Queen of England, was not in the first place an easy one. As a young man the Prince seems to have had a certain prejudice against the English, and their early reactions to him did not in any way ease his position. The House of Commons immediately reduced the annuity which it was proposed he should be given, and broadsheets were circulated in which the words " God save the King " were transcribed as " Albert de King." For a long time the Prince was made to feel a foreigner, and he never altogether lost his German accent.

There can be no question of the sincerity of his exertions on behalf of England, both in the normal course of his duties and at times of national crisis such as the Crimean War. The process of developing mutual understanding between himself and leading figures in English life was, however, a slow one, and he made a revealing comment on Anson's death when he said : " He was my only intimate friend." More-over, although he enjoyed the society of men, he was much less interested in women, and in a number of social circles this was no doubt a handicap.

These difficulties and disadvantages had the effect of making him withdraw into himself and gave him an air of aloofness, which was easily mistaken for coldness. The general state of his health may also have contributed towards producing a similar effect. Although for the greater part of his life an active and good-looking man, he was not robust, and his constitution was not of the type associated with bonhomie. If he had to stay up late at night, he suffered from an overpowering feeling of drowsiness, and much of what he did must have caused him efforts of which few people were aware. In the end he died at the early age of forty-two from what seems to have been typhoid fever, but his physical resistance was already generally undermined.

The Prince Consort's character, in short, was not one which was easily understood by his contemporaries ; indeed it was very easily misunderstood, and it must therefore continue to be puzzling to posterity. However, those who now try to examine it without prejudice may well come to the conclusion that he was a man who, the better he was known, the more he would have been respected and the more he would have been liked.

The value of his contribution to British public life is, like his character, a subject on which widely differing opinions may easily be held. One of the main causes of the bouts of unpopularity from which he periodically suffered was the very fact that he was a German. Much of the popular mistrust which he suffered on this account was no doubt caused by ignorant prejudice, but there are grounds for a serious contention that his German background unduly influenced his part in English political life.

His principal political tutor during many of his formative years was, for instance, the remarkable Baron Stockmar. Stockmar was a German doctor, who not only nearly became Foreign Minister of a united Germany, but was confidential adviser to King Leopold of the Belgians, and was at one time thought of as a possible private secretary for Queen Victoria. The Prince as a young man had been sent on a tour of Italy with Stockmar as his tutor, and after his arrival in England he frequently turned to Stockmar for advice. Stockmar was a firm believer in German unity, and the Prince shared many of his views on this subject. There was never any conflict in the Prince's mind between his duty to the country of his adoption and his interest in the unity of Germany, but it is at least arguable that, just as it may not have been to Britain's advantage that Germany became a united nation later in the century, so it would not have been to Britain's advantage if she had become united during the Prince Consort's lifetime. Such an argument, whether right or wrong, was one which the Prince Consort could hardly have admitted.

Perhaps an even better target for his critics than his tendency to sympathise too readily with German aspirations was the Prince Consort's conception of the place of the monarchy in the British constitution. Here again it is possible to trace the influence of Stockmar, who once wrote of the " absurd, usurping House of Commons." The Prince Consort held the belief that the monarch had a moral responsibility to watch over and in certain circumstances to control the Government. At barely one

Baron Stockmar

stage removed from the monarchy himself, he went some distance towards putting this belief into practice. Judged by modern standards, Palmerston's unwillingness in cases of urgency to have despatches held up for the Queen's consideration seems reasonable enough ; yet it was one of the principal causes of conflict between himself and the Court.

Of course the Prince Consort was not wholly responsible for this state of affairs. The Queen, who, like Stockmar, could declare that " the House of Commons is becoming very unmanageable and troublesome," had a will of her own and pronounced views on her rights in the conduct of foreign affairs. However, the Prince Consort, as her adviser and very much more than her adviser, was at least a joint advocate of this policy of royal intervention.

The question of the extent to which the monarch should intervene in the conduct of the nation's affairs is one of opinion. The modern form of political democracy certainly has no monopoly of good government. It is, however, undeniable that the Prince Consort's conception of the role of the monarch was far removed from that which the great majority of the British people have decided on the basis of experience to be the right one. It was, too, one which would be bound to suffer from the very unlikelihood, according to the law of averages, that a monarch or a consort would often emerge with either the general ability of Prince Albert or his capacity to render such outstanding services to his country.

The variety and extent of these services was, for a man who died at the age of forty-two, remarkable. Sir Robert Peel, between whom and the Prince Consort there was considerable natural sympathy, was the first to realise the value of giving the Prince increased opportunities for playing a leading part in public life. It was at his suggestion that the Prince became President of a Royal Commission which was appointed to consider the best means of promoting the arts and sciences in Great Britain. From the moment of that appointment onwards the Prince's public career was one of continual and varied achievement. The Royal Commission under his guidance was an exceptionally active body, and one of its more lasting and visible achievements was the founding of art galleries and museums in many parts of the country. In the field of higher education, as Chancellor of Cambridge University, and in that of social welfare, in the Society for Improving the Condition of the Labouring Classes, the Prince Consort achieved comparable results.

In addition to these duties he completely reorganised the Royal Household, so that a general state of chaos, corruption and even, it could be claimed, physical insecurity was brought to an end. He was responsible for many improvements in Army administration : he proposed reforms in the Indian Army, suggested the establishment of a training camp at Chobham, and was influential in bringing to an end the practice of duelling in the Army, an action which virtually ended duelling throughout the country. He wrote an admirable memorandum on the duties of bishops in Parliament, in which he suggested they should be less concerned with party politics than with humanitarian issues such as education, " improvement of the health of towns," " regulating factory labour " and opposing cruelty to animals. In foreign politics, apart from providing advice based on his expert knowledge of European affairs, he established a valuable personal entente with the French Emperor and, just before his death, he was influential in preventing what threatened to be a war with the United States over the affair of the steamer *Trent*.

Perhaps most important of all, the Prince Consort was largely responsible for rescuing the monarchy from the low esteem into which it had been sinking before his wife's accession to the throne, and placing it high on a basis of popular respect. The solidity of this basis has been convincingly proved by the events of the last hundred years. The Prince Consort may, in the opinion of many, have intervened too much in political affairs, but at least he understood the need for one in his position to stand above party politics. The unconcealed preference for one party which the Queen showed in the first years of her reign, and which a number of her predecessors had continually shown, ceased to be expressed once the Prince Consort began to exercise an effective influence in public affairs.

In spite of all his other accomplishments, however, the work which his contemporaries regarded as being peculiarly the Prince's own, and the one which posterity has associated with him most closely, was that of organising the Great Exhibition. The story of the Prince's part in this affair is to a large extent the story of the Exhibition itself. Some measure of his achievement is afforded by the very fact that the Great Exhibition

HER MAJESTY, as She Appeared on the FIRST of MAY, Surrounded by "Horrible Conspirators and Assassins."

The Prince Consort was largely responsible for rescuing the monarchy from the low esteem into which it had been sinking and placing it high on a basis of popular respect

of 1851 is being celebrated a hundred years later by the holding of another exhibition.   The exhibition of 1862, on the other hand, which, being staged the year after the Prince Consort's death, was thus deprived of his organising skill, is now almost completely forgotten.

CHAPTER TEN

HOW THE EXHIBITION WAS ORGANISED
AND HOW IT WAS RECEIVED

LTHOUGH the Great Exhibition eventually aroused greater popular enthusiasm than any show of its kind before or since, the history of its launching was largely one of overcoming financial and administrative difficulties as well as a good deal of active opposition. Much of the opposition proceeded from that force of inertia, which is itself commonly called conservatism, and which can sometimes attract to its support a genuine desire for conservation. Nothing comparable in scope and diversity had ever been attempted in England before. There had been local exhibitions of manufactured goods at Manchester and Birmingham, and there had been the Great Free Trade Bazaar at Covent Garden Theatre. These, however, could hardly even be considered fore-runners of what was planned for 1851, and just because it was unprecedented the proposed Great Exhibition was held by a number of people to be unwanted.

When, for instance, it was decided that the Exhibition should be staged in Hyde Park, a rallying-point for the conservative opposition was found in a number of elm-trees, whose destruction was threatened. The elms suddenly acquired a new symbolic significance and became known as " John Bull's trees of liberty." In the end a compromise on the question of their destruction was reached, and a number of the trees were left standing inside the building which housed the Exhibition. There they had the effect of attracting sparrows, whose habits seemed likely to be detrimental to the dignity of events—so detrimental indeed that, according

213

to the well-known, but not perhaps authentic, story, the matter had to be referred to the Queen, who in turn referred it to the aged Duke of Wellington, only to elicit his famous reply : " Try sparrow-hawks, ma'am." For some months, however, the Hyde Park elms did more than merely provide yet another endearing anecdote about the Duke ; they seemed to be visible pillars of resistance against dangerous innovations.

There was also an element of fear in the opposition to the proposal for a spectacle which was bound to attract large crowds, fear of an unruly mob at home and of the advent of revolutionaries from Europe. In view of the alarm which the Chartists had so recently aroused in London, and the bloodshed which had followed the revolutionary movements in many European countries, these fears, although not justified in the event, were not altogether unreasonable. By 1851 fear of mob violence had already subsided considerably. Yet when Joseph Paxton suggested that, apart from the first fortnight and one day a week subsequently, entry to the Exhibition should be free, there was an immediate storm of protest, and letters were written to the papers declaring that he had no knowledge of " the London mob." The Great Exhibition became in the end a poor man's wonder and even delight, but it was never made accessible at a poor man's price.

While inertia and fear were probably the mainsprings of the opposition, there were also a number of prominent individuals who, for various personal and other reasons, chose to be identified as antagonists of the scheme. Of these the most determined were the former Lord Chancellor, Lord Brougham, and Colonel Sibthorp, who for many years was Member of Parliament for Lincoln. Brougham had had a career of great distinction as a law reformer, an advocate of popular education and a champion of the abolition of slavery ; he had founded London University and had been a spirited defender of the cause of Queen Caroline. By the time of the Exhibition, however, he was already in his seventies, and he had suffered a serious decline in public regard and also, it seems, in his powers of judgment. More than two years before the Exhibition was held, *The Times* wrote of him : " Lord Brougham has great powers, and had once a great name. He has spoilt both the one and the other. His powers are out of his control, and his name is beyond recovery. . . . There is only the disappointment of a man who lived for popularity and then outlived it." Disraeli confirmed this judgment when he described Brougham as " an extinct volcano."

Brougham was regarded by contemporaries as the champion of those householders—one of whom was his brother—whose view over Hyde Park would be spoilt by the Exhibition. This consideration may have

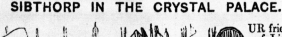

SIBTHORP IN THE CRYSTAL PALACE.

UR friends the citizens of Lincoln have good right to a peculiar pride in their great political TOM—the wise COL. SIBTHORP. He is in the present Session as deep and as clear as usual. We are told that the old bell, called the Tom of Lincoln, became cracked in 1827; but though Lincoln's political TOM,

"Swinging slow, with sullen roar,"

has, for many a year, given thundering note of warning and alarm to the whole country, *that* TOM is, in the present Session of 1851, as sound as ever—quite. On the first day of Parliament, COLONEL TOM tolled thus, in the affrighted ears of the architect of the Crystal Palace :—

" They might call it success, but he called it failure. He did not wish to see that building destroyed by any acts of violence, but would to GOD that some hailstorm, or some visitation of lightning, might descend to defeat the ill-advised project."

Sibthorp was one of those eloquent diehards, of whom at least one
outstanding example is commonly found in the House of Commons

influenced him, but stronger motives of his own were probably his personal antagonism to the Prince Consort and his increasing tendency to become an advocate of lost causes. In any case he did not quite reach the fervour of opposition shown by Colonel Sibthorp. Sibthorp was one of those eloquent diehards, of whom at least one outstanding example is commonly found in the House of Commons. He had opposed Catholic emancipation, he had opposed railway bills on principle because he disliked railways, he had opposed parliamentary reform, and he had opposed free trade. Having suffered one defeat after another on these issues, he found in the proposal to hold an exhibition a new and powerful stimulus. On grounds of logic, he called attention to the danger of an invasion of Papists and the establishment of brothels by foreigners in South Kensington ; and on grounds of piety, he expressed the hope that hail or lightning might descend from Heaven to show the Almighty's displeasure with the whole affair.

Such active opposition as there was, however, remained confined to a minority, whose opinions carried less and less weight as popular enthusiasm grew. In any case it gave the organisers of the Exhibition much less concern than their continual administrative and financial difficulties. The expedient of having a sum of money adequate for all needs voted out of public funds by an acquiescent parliament was not available to them. They had instead to persuade a sufficient number of individuals and firms that the project merited support.

The decision to throw the Exhibition open to the whole civilised world also gave rise to special problems. A number of foreign exhibitors showed a distressing lack of a sense of urgency in their preparations, the dilatoriness of Belgium, Russia and Turkey, in particular, giving cause for alarm. There was, too, a constant danger of offending national susceptibilities in the division of floor space. Not only did Spain and Portugal surprise certain well-meaning but perhaps slightly ignorant British officials by insisting on exhibiting separately, but similar divisions had to be made between the exhibitors from Sardinia, Rome and Tuscany.

Finally there was the task of choosing a suitable architect and design for the building. This task proved to be much more difficult than had been expected. Although between two hundred and two hundred and fifty designs were originally submitted, the members of the Building Committee were not satisfied by any of them, and they decided instead to produce a design of their own. In doing so they were accused, not unreasonably, of stealing a great many ideas from the other designs they had studied and producing a not very inspiring result. The indignation aroused was widespread and outspoken.

One after another, however, these various difficulties were overcome.

The Society of Arts under the guidance of Prince Albert did not waver in its support of the whole project, and, as a result of visits by its members to manufacturing districts, a satisfactory response from industrialists was evoked. A banquet given by the Lord Mayor of London in November, 1849, served to arouse further interest, and gradually personal guarantees

Among the most regular visitors was the Duke of Wellington, then in his eighty-second year

against any losses which might be incurred were forthcoming, in one case the guarantee being for as much as £50,000. Serious international incidents were also avoided, although sundry complaints continued to be voiced until the end. Thus, when the awards were finally announced, there were protests from many quarters : one French critic, for instance, stated that only in those fields in which there was no serious competition with British goods were first prizes awarded to French exhibitors. The dangers of public disturbance were guarded against by resisting the proposal to allow free entry ; by forbidding the sale of any alcohol in the refreshment rooms ; and by a decision to augment the City and Metropolitan Police force by 900 men. The most spectacular triumph of all, however, was the ultimate choice of a building to house the Exhibition, the building which became known as the Crystal Palace.

Joseph Paxton, the designer of the Crystal Palace, was for many years the Duke of Devonshire's gardener. As an architect Paxton was entirely self-taught, but he was a man of exceptional and varied gifts. He was the son of a Bedfordshire farmer and left home to become a gardener. The Duke of Devonshire first met him while walking from his house in Chiswick through the gardens of the Horticultural Society, where Paxton was employed. The Duke was impressed by Paxton's intelligence and decided to appoint him head gardener at Chatsworth, although Paxton at the time was only twenty-three years old.

The duties which Paxton accepted one after another at Chatsworth were far beyond those normally expected of a gardener. He organised the dispatch of a botanical expedition to the Pacific coast of North America ; planned a model village at Edensor near Chatsworth ; accompanied the Duke on a seven-months' tour of Europe ; and organised the Duke's entertainment of the Emperor Nicholas of Russia. For this last feat of management he was created a Knight of St. Vladimir. He also undertook many other activities less directly connected with his work at Chatsworth. He grew rich by railway speculation and became a director of the Midland Railway ; he was a co-founder of the *Daily News*, of which Charles Dickens became the first editor ; and he was a member of a commission, which was appointed to report on Kew Gardens, and which advocated their retention for the nation.

Gardens and buildings were always among his principal interests, and he indulged his taste for both by constructing the Chatsworth conservatory in 1840. This was at the time the largest glass building in the world. Contemporaries compared it, somewhat curiously, with St. Peter's in Rome, and they were particularly impressed by the fact that a carriage and pair could be driven down the main aisle.

Paxton's experiments in glass buildings reached their culmination in the Crystal Palace. He did, it is true, later in his life put forward a plan

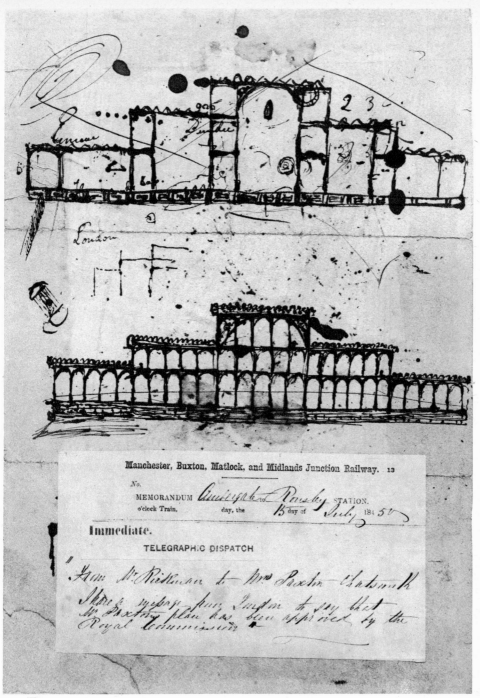

Paxton made the original sketch of the Crystal Palace on blotting-paper during a board meeting of the Midland Railway Company in Derby

for a Great Victorian Way round London, which was to be made of iron and roofed with glass, and which would carry eight railway lines as well as shops and houses. However, it remained only a plan, and it was on the Crystal Palace that his fame was to rest.

The story is now well known of the way in which Paxton had his plan for the Exhibition building accepted : how he made the original sketch on blotting-paper during a board meeting of the Midland Railway Company in Derby ; how he gained the interest of Robert Stephenson ; and how he appealed to the public over the heads of the Building Committee of the Exhibition by publishing his plans in the *Illustrated London News*. The judges were won over to approving his plans with remarkable suddenness, and Douglas Jerrold, writing in *Punch*, had the happy idea of naming the building " Crystal Palace."

The Crystal Palace rapidly received recognition as a masterpiece. It was magnificent, it was novel, and it was indisputably functional ; and the popular reaction to the building was an assurance of the ultimate success of the Exhibition. The construction of the Crystal Palace was a triumph of what may well be called mass production. The contractors were continually working against time : new ideas were adopted, such as having the glaziers working in small covered carriages which travelled along the gutters ; there were setbacks, as when a thousand square feet of glazing were blown away in a gale ; and there were alarming doubts about the solidity of various parts of the structure. To satisfy these doubts it was decided to hold a parade of sappers, who were made to mark time in the most testing fashion possible. It had been found that the contractors' men, with whom the experiment was first tried, were not very good at going through military motions. At the end of the sappers' parade, eminent scientists who had witnessed it declared that " at the climax of vibration the motion did not exceed that common in ordinary London houses at evening parties."

All these anxieties, however, only increased popular interest in the Crystal Palace. That it should be ready in time was regarded almost as a national challenge, and, in spite of the entrance fee which was charged, visiting the building in the course of construction became a favourite pastime. Among the most regular visitors was the Duke of Wellington, then in his eighty-second year, and on one of the last days on which the

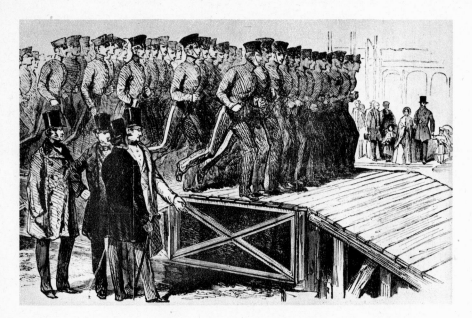

Sappers were made to mark time in the most testing fashion

public were admitted before the Exhibition began, a sum of more than £100 was taken at the door.

This interest in the Crystal Palace reflected a wider enthusiasm for the whole Exhibition, an enthusiasm which steadily drowned the diminishing number of disapproving voices, and which mounted continuously as the early months of the year 1851 passed, and the opening day, May 1st, drew near.

The occasion of the Exhibition provided an opportunity for many kinds of enthusiasts to advance proposals on what should be done to celebrate the great event. It was suggested, for instance, that a towering column, to be paid for by a public subscription, should be erected in London in honour of the Queen and Prince Albert. A clergyman's wife advocated the establishment of a cookery school, which should accept only girls with good references from their former employers or the clergyman of their parish ; these girls could then help to remedy the shortage of good cooks from which visitors to the Exhibition might suffer, " their

SCENE—EXHIBITION REFRESHMENT ROOM.

Visitor. "PINT O' BEER, MISS, PLEASE."

Miss. "DON'T KEEP IT. YOU CAN HAVE A STRAWBERRY ICE AND A WAFER!"

The sale of alcohol in the refreshment rooms was forbidden

services being gratuitous to their employers and merely instructive to themselves." In a letter to *The Times* it was pointed out that in the matter of " temporary conveniences " London was the worst provided city in Europe ; the writer suggested that this deficiency should be made good before the Exhibition was opened, as " foreigners are not particular when certain calls of nature press, where they stop to relieve themselves." Another idea was that there should " everywhere appear on perpendicular faces of ribs and stouter supports " within the Exhibition building the

RATHER ALARMING; Or, HOTELS IN 1851.

No. 7.—Frenchman. "MADEMOISELLE ! MES BOTTES, S'IL VOUS PLAIT ! "
No. 10.—Italian. "SIGNORA, AVRÒ IO L'ACQUA CALDA STA MANE ? "
No. 6.—German. "WO IST MEIN SODA WASSER ? "

Hotels in 1851

A HINT TO THE COMMISSIONERS.

"Mon Dieu, Alphonse! Regardez-donc. Comment appele-t-on cette Machine-là?"
"Tiens, c'est drôle—mais je ne sais pas."

Frenchman and wash-basin

words, "Glory to God in the highest, and on earth peace, goodwill toward men." The precedent cited for this innovation was that of the Saracenic inscriptions in the Alhambra.

None of these proposals was considered sufficiently appropriate to be put into effect. Nor was the more modest suggestion that the Commissioners should provide lodgings for visiting artisans, as it was thought that such action would be an unwarranted interference with private enterprise. There were, however, many new activities to which the Exhibition gave rise, varying in nature from the staging of a horse-race for the Great Exhibition Plate at Epsom to the offer of a hundred guineas prize at Oxford University for the best essay on the subject : " In what respect is the union of all nations at the Great Exhibition calculated to further the moral and religious welfare of mankind ? "

This was a question to which time has not yet provided a clear answer, although the most immediate outcome of the international nature of the Exhibition was a lavish entertainment staged by the Municipality of Paris for the Lord Mayor of London and the City Corporation. *The Times* considered this gesture so ill-chosen that it declared : " What do the Lord Mayor and Corporation of London represent but jobbery and good living, not to say gluttony and corruption ? "

The most splendid occasion of the year was, however, the opening ceremony. The Queen appeared dressed in pink and gold brocade ; Prince Albert read an address to the Queen on behalf of the Commissioners ; the Queen declared the Exhibition open; and the *Hallelujah Chorus* was sung by massed choirs to the accompaniment of massed bands. The effect of this chorus was not as overwhelming as might be thought, for, according to a contemporary observer, such was the extent of the Crystal Palace that at its extremities the sound was " similar to that of a musical snuff-box." Thackeray, on the other hand, recorded a somewhat different impression in lines, whose majesty is to-day a little tarnished by the association of words :

> " *The fountain in the basin plays,*
> *The chanting organ echoes clear,*
> *An awful chorus 'tis to hear,*
> *A wondrous song !* "

The feelings of many people on the occasion were, however, most aptly summed up by the Queen when she wrote : " The only event it in the slightest degree reminded me of was the Coronation, but this day's festival was a thousand times superior." May 1st was, she declared, " the *greatest* day in our history," and the spectacle was " the most *beautiful* and *imposing* and *touching* . . . ever seen, and the triumph of my beloved Albert."

Photograph of the Queen opening the Crystal Palace at Sydenham

Once the Exhibition had been thrown open to the public, people came from all parts of the country to see it. The railway companies were forced to reduce fares, particularly from the north of England, where they were faced with the competition of cheap sea-trips from Hull. The price of the return railway excursion trip from the West Riding to London was eventually brought down to five shillings. Agricultural labourers, under the guidance of their clergymen, arrived in London wearing what contemporaries called "peasant's attire," and an old woman of eighty-five walked the whole way from Penzance with a basket on her head for the express purpose of seeing the Exhibition. Cabs became difficult to find, and there was such a shortage of accommodation that one indignant visitor complained that he had had to pay seven guineas a week for lodgings in Welbeck Street, only to be continually bitten by bugs. The newspapers for a long time treated the Exhibition as one of the principal items of the day's news. *The Times* devoted a column or a paragraph to it every day for months, recording the number of visitors, listing the important personages among them, or adding new reflections on the exhibits themselves and their possible effects on the working classes.

The total number of visitors was 6,201,856. During the closing weeks the crowds became larger than ever before, in spite of the

Mary Callinack, aged eighty-five, walked from Penzance to the Great Exhibiton

rain which poured incessantly on the last day on which visitors were admitted for a shilling. At one particular moment, 2 p.m. on October 27th, 92,000 people were recorded as having been inside the building together.

The conduct of these huge crowds was remarkably orderly. The number of offences committed inside the building for which charges were made was twenty-five, nine being for picking pockets, six for attempting to pick pockets, and ten for petty larceny at the stalls. Yet 42 purses with cash ranging in amounts from 1s. 3d. to £6 10s., 423 parcels, 93 bracelets, 17 rings, 16 watches and £28 2s. 6d. in loose cash were returned to their owners. Nearly as many articles were handed in to officials but remained unclaimed.

Underlying the popular enthusiasm and the general sense of responsibility which the Exhibition engendered, there was, however, a widespread feeling of regret. This was aroused by the expectation of a serious public loss. The Crystal Palace was designed as a temporary structure, for the Commissioners had given an undertaking that once the Exhibition was closed the site would be cleared.

The idea that this building, which had delighted so many millions, must disappear after six months was not of course accepted readily, and a powerful movement grew up for the Crystal Palace's retention. There were numerous letters to the press on the subject. A doctor wrote to *The Times*, pointing out the advantages of retaining the Crystal Palace as a winter garden, as it would encourage people to take exercise, and advocating the installation of the waters of all the leading spas. In another letter it was stated that ten people out of eleven in London wanted the building to be retained, and the writer declared : " Neither can I imagine that the noble Prince . . . would willingly consent to raze to the ground one of the noblest monuments of the greatness of our country, which will form an epoch in the annals of England, and of the world." Paxton announced that the Crystal Palace could be put into condition for permanent use at a cost of between £12,000 and £15,000, and that no public grant would be needed to raise this sum. Petitions against the removal of the Crystal Palace were presented in the House of Lords from places as far away as Stockport, and after a debate in the House of Commons there were seventy-five votes in favour of its retention until May 1st, 1852, and only forty-seven against. In spite of all these expressions of opinion, however, the Commissioners decided that their undertaking must be honoured, and the Crystal Palace in Hyde Park was doomed.

Although the Crystal Palace had to be removed from Hyde Park, it did not of course disappear. A private company was formed, of which Paxton was one of the leading spirits, and the building was transported to Sydenham Hill, where it was re-erected in a somewhat different form. There it remained as a centre of entertainment—particularly band contests and fireworks—until it was destroyed by fire in 1936. In its later years it revealed some of the limitations of glass as a material for permanent buildings, but it was always a noble monument. To-day the name " Crystal Palace " survives as a memory, and as the name of a football club and of a terminus for some of the London bus routes.

The Great Exhibition inspired writers of tracts and hymns ; it became a familiar subject for decoration in a wide variety of media ranging from embroidery to inlaid mother-of-pearl ; and it was an event which even Lord Palmerston, who, when it was launched, was in the middle of one of his major conflicts with Prince Albert, described as the most significant he had lived to witness. Yet its permanent effects are not altogether easy to trace. It did not, as was hoped, lead to an era of peace between the nations, for it was shortly followed by the only European war in which Victorian England was involved. Its principal effect on design was perhaps to create a reaction against what were supposed to be its masterpieces : a new generation was growing up which was to adopt strikingly different standards, and William Morris, visiting the Exhibition at the age of seventeen, was appalled by its general ugliness. The Exhibition may indeed have influenced the promotion of mass entertainment, the growth of imperialism, and the technique of salesmanship, but whether it did so to any significant extent is in each case debatable.

There are, however, certain memorials to the Exhibition which have survived, and they are in themselves consequences of the way in which the finances of the enterprise were handled. Unlike many later international exhibitions, the Exhibition of 1851 showed a substantial profit balance. After considerable discussion, it was decided that the profits should be devoted to various projects for the promotion of the arts and sciences. To this decision we owe both the existence of a science museum in South Kensington and, as a consequence of the manner in which the

PRAISE AND PUDDING.

H.R.H. *Pr-nce Albert.*—"Master Joseph Paxton—In Addition to the Honours that have been heaped upon You, I have much Pleasure in Presenting You with this Piece of 'Solid Pudding.'"

The exhibition showed a substantial profit balance

profits of the Exhibition were invested, certain valuable scholarships which are still awarded to-day.

As a result of the Exhibition, therefore, what may be considered a new quarter of London was developed, for to an existing quarter a wholly new character was given. That part of London, some of which falls in the City of Westminster and some in the Borough of Kensington, and which is traversed by a thoroughfare very properly known as Exhibition Road, is to-day served by an underground station carrying the sign : " South Kensington. For Museums." It is the world to which Wells's Ann Veronica escaped from a suburb not far from the Crystal Palace in search of spiritual freedom, the world of which a Swiss guide-book recently stated that it was " placé sous le double signe de la respectabilité bourgeoise et de la science officielle." Whatever may be thought of its architecture, it is a quarter which any serious estate agent would to-day classify as one of the most desirable residential areas of London. It is perhaps the most satisfying enduring monument to the Great Exhibition and its creator, the Prince Consort.

CHAPTER ELEVEN

THE EXHIBITION ITSELF

SO SUCCESSFUL were the organisers of the Great Exhibition in arousing the interest of manufacturers and of enterprising individual craftsmen that in the end more than 15,000 exhibitors participated. Their goods were displayed along a frontage of more than ten miles with a lavishness which understandably dazzled spectators who had never seen anything comparable in magnificence before.

The first objects to attract the attention of the visitor arriving at the Crystal Palace offered a fair sample of that mixture of the ornately decorative and the exclusively utilitarian, which pervaded every section of the Exhibition. These objects were the exhibits placed outside the building, the statuary and other forms of decoration in the main avenues and, as loyalty demanded in many cases, the contributions from the Royal Family. Of the royal exhibits one which provoked special admiration was, in the words of the catalogue, " a cradle, carved in Turkey boxwood, symbolising the union of the Royal House of England with that of Saxe-Coburg and Gotha. One end exhibits in the centre the armorial bearings of Her Majesty the Queen, surrounded by masses of foliage, natural flowers and birds ; on the rocker, beneath, is seen the head of ' Nox,' represented as a beautiful sleeping female, crowned with a garland of poppies, supported upon bats' wings, and surrounded by the seven planets." Outside the building there was a single 24-ton block of coal, and, in one of the main avenues, a remarkable juxtaposition of statuary representing the Madonna and Child and a sheet of galvanised tinned iron.

232

Aerial view of the Crystal Palace

After viewing these objects, visitors normally began their tour of the main exhibits by turning into the western half of the Crystal Palace. Here they found the products of the British Empire. The eastern half of the building was given up to foreign countries, whose sites were allotted, in order to avoid recriminations, on what purported to be a geographic basis.

The British exhibits, apart from the products of the colonies, were divided into four main sections : raw materials, machinery, manufactures, and sculpture and the fine arts.

Of the raw materials a high proportion consisted, very properly, of mining and mineral products. Coal, on whose extraction most of the wealth displayed in the Exhibition was in the first instance based, was given due prominence. A novelty in the class for mining and mineral products which might, however, have aroused the interest of the visitor was guano, whose exhibitor found it necessary, in view of its rarity, to describe as " a superior fertiliser."

In the class for chemical and pharmaceutical products, an appreciation of enlightened medical opinion was shown by the inclusion of cod liver oil ; and the art of furnishers and decorators was represented by a chemical used for imparting a mahogany and rosewood colour to common woods. There were also novelties in the form of matches made with amorphous phosphorus, which were said to be " free from offensive smell " and " to give out a brilliant and sure light, when rubbed on the sanded part of the box." Luxuries included an elixir of sarsaparilla.

In the class for substances used as food, certain limitations were imposed by the decision to exclude alcoholic drinks almost completely from the exhibits as well as completely from the refreshment rooms. In the case of exhibits, the only exceptions made were in favour of drinks derived from unusual sources. One exhibitor conformed with both the the letter and the spirit of this regulation by displaying what he called champagne, which was manufactured in England from rhubarb stalks. Of the other exhibits of foodstuffs, a somewhat curious one was a canister of boiled mutton, which had been supplied for an Arctic expedition, and which had been discovered in 1849, twenty-five years later, in an allegedly perfect state of preservation.

On the whole, the raw materials of Great Britain did not form one

The interior of the Crystal Palace

of the most interesting categories of exhibits. This in itself reflected the growing belief that the provision of raw materials was primarily a function of colonial dependencies. A more interesting section was that of machinery. Those of us to-day who study the illustrations in the catalogue and in contemporary journals may well come to the conclusion that this section contained the most elegant exhibits of all in the form of carriages. It was an age in which work of considerable distinction in the art of carriage-building was achieved. Only eight years before the Exhibition was held, Joseph Aloysius Hansom had patented his cab, and in the catalogue the name of one of the principal opponents of the whole Exhibition was nevertheless commemorated by the entry, " a four-wheeled carriage or improved brougham."

Many of the other exhibits of means of transport were representative of the railway rather than the carriage era. They included a plan of a locomotive steam engine " for common roads," a model of a suspension bridge for a railway between England and France—a project which the exhibitor could hardly have expected to remain unfulfilled a hundred years later—and a model of London with a design for railways in the streets.

Among the classes for manufacturing machines and tools, and for civil engineering, architectural and building contrivances, there were a number of highly original exhibits. These included a railway break calculated to prevent collision and to act without a shock ; a refrigerator for condensing steam ; a patent submarine helmet and other diving apparatus ; a model of the proposed grand ship canal through the isthmus of Suez ; and what the catalogue, with a suggestion of philanthropy, described as a " window-cleaner, for the protection of female servants from fatal accidents and public exposure."

In the naval and military exhibits, there was an intimation of the future in a model of a rocket apparatus, and a suggestion of more leisurely methods of warfare in a collapsible seat which could be carried in the pocket. This class, also, somewhat surprisingly, included a ladies' bathing-machine.

The class for " philosophical, musical, horological and surgical instruments " was perhaps that which offered the greatest opportunities for the inventive skill of the age. There was a wide variety of models

Some of the most elegant exhibits were the carriages

of flying-machines, ranging from embryonic aeroplanes to a " self-propelling rotatory balloon." There were " electric printing telegraphs " and an electric table-lamp described as " suitable for a room." Clocks extended in range from a new kind of alarm, characteristically called a " servant's regulator," to one " showing the days of the month, months of the year, the motions of the sun and moon, and the state of tide at some of the principal seaports of Great Britain, Ireland, France, America, Spain, Portugal, Holland and Germany, and going for twelve months." Considerable ingenuity was shown, too, in appliances for remedying human deficiencies. Among these were artificial teeth, artificial legs and even an artificial silver nose. There were also elastic chest-expanders and a garment happily styled a " corset à tous ressorts." All these remarkable inventions being on view, it comes as rather a shock to discover that amongst them were bleeding instruments, which were described in the catalogue as " substitutes for leeches."

The third category of British goods, that of manufactures was, like the section for machinery, an extensive and varied one. Among the woollen and worsted goods there were indications of the trends of international trade in the display of different kinds of cloth for the home market and for the American, Chinese and Russian markets ; but the dependence of English manufacturers on Australian and German wool was also evident.

In the class which included leather and skins, different social strata were catered for by the display of artificial hair and of " clogs, as worn by the operatives of Lancashire and Yorkshire." The paper, printing and bookbinding class included two somewhat unsuccessful attempts to meet needs which were later to be satisfied by the typewriter and the Braille system. These were a " portable letter-case, for taking copies of letters, written in ink, by the mere pressure of the hand," and " tangible ink for the blind, producing raised characters on paper."

In the tapestry, lace and embroidery class, utility was for the most part submerged in a riot of personal fancy. Among the most remarkable exhibits in this class were a carpet worked for the benefit of the Society for Promoting the Scriptural Education of the Native Irish ; an infant's knitted robe consisting of 1,464,859 stitches and 6,300 yards of cotton ; and, possibly for the edification of foreign visitors, a design provocatively entitled " Le Vendredi: a Catholic family eating meat on Friday."

The hardware class was predominantly utilitarian and contained work of striking originality. There were a number of gas-cooking stoves, one of which, it was claimed, could provide meals for a hundred persons ; there was a model of a shower-bath ; a washing and mangling machine ; " a patent oven, having the heating apparatus within " ; and an ingenious device described as an " alarm lock ; on an attempt being made to pick it, a bell rings, and when the bolt is shot a pistol is fired." Another exhibit, whose significance for the future is evident enough to-day, was modestly listed as " specimens of steel suitable for engineering."

The class containing works in precious metals and jewellery was perhaps somewhat out of place among the other manufactures. The spirit which dominated it was essentially that of the fine arts section. Silver in particular was used as a medium for the representation in minute detail of heroic, exotic and legendary events. Groups in silver represented Sir Roger de Coverley with the Gipsies, and Arab merchants halting in the desert ; the battle of Alexander and Darius was portrayed on a chased shield ; and the labours of Hercules appeared on a silver salver.

A similar spirit, with an even greater licence for fantasy, was evident in the furniture class. No other age could have produced " a commode of various woods, the panels ornamented with marqueterie and carvings, and painted china in the centre ; the whole finished with rich gilt mould-ings, etc." Almost the only relief from the overwhelming in this class came from the manifestation of another characteristic of the period, the belief in encouraging the industrious artisan. Of the millions of visitors who inspected the furniture, many were no doubt gratified to note that a certain carved book-tray was " executed by a ploughman, in the evening, by candle-light, without the aid of any model or design, and solely with a penknife."

The final class of the manufactures was properly labelled " miscel-laneous." It would have been difficult to find any other title for a class which included a device called the euxesis for shaving without soap or water ; a bird-cage containing 2,522 pieces and composed of twenty-one different kinds of wood ; and a " stiletto or defensive umbrella."

The sculpture and fine arts revealed many of those qualities and talents, of which the other exhibits had already provided such overwhelming evidence. Chief of these qualities were a remarkable facility for discovering new processes of manufacture, and a corresponding determination to make use of them irrespective of the æsthetic consequences. Considerable technical advances had, for instance, been made a short time before in the art of printing in colours. Indeed people were beginning to advance the claim that prints of pictures could even be compared favourably with good daguerreotypes, thus providing an early example of the belief that some paintings could be almost as good as

Professor Kiss's Amazon group

photographs. The talent for invention and the delight in the unorthodox being what they were, the fine arts and sculpture section contained work executed in a remarkable variety of media. There were daguerreotype portraits and electrotype casts ; there was engraving on charred chestnut-wood ; pyrography executed on a lime-tree with a red-hot poker ; and what the exhibitor described as a new type of painting, consisting of the " application of finely-pulverised colour to a granulated oil-ground." Views were carved inside egg-shells ; the Lord's Prayer was written in twenty-six different styles of illuminated letters ; and a model of St. Paul's was made from cardboard with a penknife.

In spite of this widespread talent for technical innovation, there was a marked absence of inspiration or originality in the choice and, indeed, in the artistic treatment of subjects. The standard classical themes, such as Cupid in a variety of situations and the parting of Hector and Andromache, recurred relentlessly. So did scenes from Shakespeare and Milton, heroic literary and historical events, and the romance of the Scottish Highlands. So, too, did slightly suggestive statues of bathers, which were duly offset by other pieces portraying " Innocence." Where modern events and personages provided the subjects, the results tended to be even more unfortunate. There was one particularly desolating statue of the future King Edward VII as a young shepherd ; Queen Victoria was made to look almost equally ill at ease on a charger ; and there was a design for a national monument to Prince Albert, which may well have suggested some ideas for the celebrated memorial which was erected after his death. In this design there were to be four large bronze panel castings—twice the size of those at the base of Nelson's column—showing scenes from the Exhibition, with Europe, Asia, Africa and America as " emblematical figures " seated on piers at the four angles of the base. Above there was to be a globe surmounted by a marble statue of the Prince.

In spite of the opulence and ostentation which the fine arts and the manufactures of the United Kingdom revealed, it was nevertheless from the exhibits of the colonies that many British visitors to the Exhibition received their most vivid impression of riches. These were riches, more-over, of which they felt themselves to be in a sense part-proprietors. The greatest display of colonial wealth was that afforded by the products of the East Indies. They included iron, copper, lead and tin ores ; gold, antimony and cinnabar ; agates, chalcedony, bloodstones and lapis lazuli ; wheat, flour, oats, rice, millets and pulses ; tea and coffee, tobacco and opium ; spices, sugar and oils ; indigo and other dyes ; collections of woods, of which some numbered more than a hundred specimens ; silks, ivory and pearls ; and numerous manufactures, of which the most magnificent were the jewels. Among the jewels was the wonderful Duria-i-noor or Sea of Light diamond, but many visitors were even more impressed by the glass model which was on show of the great Koh-i-noor itself.

The other colonies, too, had their wealth displayed, and British visitors to the Exhibition became aware that their country had such possessions as Malta and the Ionian Islands in the Mediterranean, New Brunswick and the Falkland Islands in the New World, the Gold Coast and Mauritius, Van Diemen's Land and New Zealand. The first signs of the industrialisation of these territories might have been noticed in such isolated exhibits as model locomotives from Canada, but for the most part the contribution of the colonies consisted of raw materials. Some were familiar, some were less well known, and among the less familiar and probably less noted products was one listed in the catalogue as " ground nuts, from which oil is extracted."

Of the foreign exhibits, those of the United States could be regarded as in some respects forming a bridge between the colonial contributions and the contributions of the industrialised European countries. The proportion of what were known as colonial products among the American exhibits, such as maple sugar, tobacco and preserved peaches, was certainly very high. However, it was not this aspect of the American contribution, but rather the nature of their industrial products, which made the strongest impression on contemporary visitors. An English newspaper, for instance, commented that the American " industrial system . . . is essentially democratic in its tendencies. They produce for the masses, and for a wholesale consumption." Of the individual American exhibits, the one which aroused the most general admiration was Power's provocative statue of a Greek slave. Mr. Colt's revolvers were also noted with interest, and surprise was expressed that they did not win any award.

Americans in London, aware of the prestige which a good national

The greatest display of colonial wealth was that afforded by the East Indies

Floating church for seamen at Philadelphia

contribution would confer in the eyes of Englishmen, complained that the United States Congress, contrary to the practice of a number of Governments, was unwilling to vote any money out of public funds to assist would-be exhibitors. They pointed out that the American showing must suffer in consequence. What did in fact happen was that some of the floor space which had originally been allotted to American exhibitors, but which they could not fill, was given up to certain British and French firms which had been crowded out of the space assigned to their own countries. In spite of this, the contribution of the United States was much larger and more impressive than that of the other independent

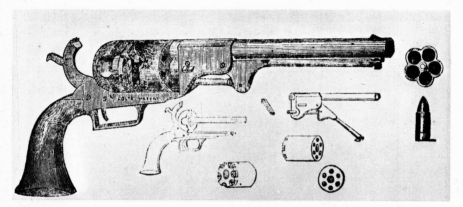

Mr. Colt's revolvers were noted with interest

American nations. The sole contribution from Chile was a lump of gold weighing three hundredweight, and of the four Brazilian exhibits, the most striking was a bouquet of flowers made of the feathers of birds native to the country, " with the exception of a few made of beetles' wings."

The French contribution was considerably larger than that of any other foreign country. Their porcelain, tapestry and textiles were widely admired, as was some of the Algerian fancy cabinet work. In the field of electricity there were some important exhibits, such as " Volta-electric apparatus, and double-current magneto-electric apparatus." There were also a number of useful domestic novelties, such as patent spring mattresses and patent concentrated milk ; it was considered permissible to include both peach and apricot brandy in the limited alcoholic field ; and there was an interesting departure in the direction of naturalism in a marble statue of a billiard player.

The Austrian exhibits reflected the heterogeneous nature of the Empire, and racial minorities were strongly represented. There was a fez ; there was Milanese statuary ; there was Bohemian glass ; there were Hungarian national dresses ; and there were " caps of various countries, including Nisam, Mezidic, Servian and Polish." There was also a zither—it was found necessary to explain to the British public that this was a stringed instrument—and the most extravagant English essays in the ornate were challenged by a " tableau representing the capture of King Porus ; with 217 figures embossed by hand on a plate of silver weighing 18 marks 3 ounces."

Russia was confronted with continual difficulties in presenting a satisfactory contribution. The worst of these was that a ship bringing many of the exhibits was ice-bound in the Baltic. In the end it was the exotic nature of many of the Russian goods, the leopard, tiger and pelican skins, the Cossack armour and the jasper and gilt vases, which aroused the greatest interest. There was one other curious Russian item which did not feature in the collections of other nations. This was exhibited by a peasant, and was described somewhat cryptically in the catalogue as " portable soup."

Of the German exhibits, those of the states of the Zollverein were declared by *The Times* to approach " more nearly a utilitarian standard than the majority of our foreign contributors." A mild reproach seems to have been implied in this comment, but some alarm may also have been felt at the high proportion of industrial products which these potential competitors displayed. One German exhibit which does not seem to have aroused great interest at the time was listed as "Krupp, F., Essen, near the Ruhr. Steel gun, 6-pounder, complete."

For the rest, the wood-carving, mosaics and sculpture from a number of the Italian states, the blades from Toledo, the lace from Belgium—a country which also somewhat surprisingly exhibited tobacco—and the products of the marble quarries which had been reopened in Greece helped to complete the picture of the riches and magnificence of all the

Lifeguards outside the Crystal Palace

world. One other exhibit also calls for comment. This was from Switzerland, and it was listed in the catalogue as " a gold watch, size about one inch." Amidst the general display of splendour, it was remarkable in that its exhibitor claimed as a distinction the fact that it was small.

" Hideous " is an epithet which later generations have frequently applied to the wares displayed at the Great Exhibition, and there is no doubt that much of what was on show—and indeed admired and subsequently imitated—was executed in what posterity has agreed to stigmatise as abominable taste. Contemporary opinion was not, however, as oblivious of the shortcomings of the general standard of design as is commonly supposed, and others besides William Morris expressed their disapproval. *The Times*, commenting on the contribution from the United States, declared that " they, like us, have everything to learn in matters of design. They have inherited our ignorance on that subject, and increased it by vulgarities peculiarly their own." There was also a good deal of criticism of the standards adopted by the juries which awarded the prizes. Some of this was, no doubt, inspired by envy, as in the case of the enamel painter who publicly proclaimed that it was a " palpable injustice " that he had received no award, but much of it was rather more appropriate. The fundamental misconception underlying the continual emphasis on decoration did not pass unnoticed ; a speaker who took part in a series of lectures on the Exhibition, for example, suggested that more attention should be paid to the working parts of agricultural steam engines and less to their external ornament. Above all, the very spirit of the Exhibition was called into question in a pastoral letter from Cardinal Wiseman, in which he advocated " laying up blessing and grace . . . to avert any evils which may result from this national display of greatness."

Nevertheless, critics who voiced such opinions formed a distinguished minority. The great majority of the crowds who thronged the Crystal Palace delighted above all in the magnificent, the costly and the immense. The Koh-i-noor model, the crystal fountain, Professor Kiss's Amazon group, the Milanese stained-glass windows, the largest mirror in the world, and Marochetti's gigantic statue of Richard Cœur-de-Lion— these were the exhibits which day after day drew large and enraptured crowds. Their quality must, in a number of cases, be a matter of opinion ;

Marochetti's gigantic statue of Richard Cœur-de-Lion

of their sumptuousness there can be no doubt. They expressed and symbolised a feeling which was put into words by the Archbishop of Canterbury in his prayer at the opening ceremony when, making apt use of a familiar quotation, he stated that " peace is within our walls and plenteousness within our palaces."

The Archbishop was, of course, quite right in both his claims. What was most revealing about the character of the age was the fact that these claims could be made with so little fear of contradiction. The same words could hardly be uttered with the same equanimity to-day, when we are celebrating the centenary of the Great Exhibition ; nor would they have seemed altogether appropriate in many of the intervening years. There perhaps, if anywhere, is to be found the fundamental difference, not so much in material conditions as in mental attitude, which distinguishes the age of 1851 from the ages which have succeeded it.

THE END

INDEX